Keep It Good

Understanding Creation Care
through Parables

C. LINDSAY LINSKY, PHD

Copyright Notice

The Scripture quotations contained herein are from the New Revised Standard Version Bible, copyright © 1989 by the Division of Christian Education of the National Council of the Churches of Christ in the U.S.A. Used by permission. All rights reserved.

Keep It Good: Understanding Creation Care through Parables, © 2016 by Catherine Lindsay Linsky. All rights reserved. With the exception of brief excerpts for review purpose, no part of this book may be reproduced in any manner whatsoever without written permission from the author. For information or questions about use of copyrighted material please visit www.keepitgood.org for contact information.

Printed in the United States of America.

Library of Congress Cataloging-in-Publication Data

Linsky, Catherine Lindsay

Keep it good: Understanding creation care through parables / Lindsay Linsky.
>   p. cm.
>   ISBN 978-0-9975909-0-6

To order additional copies of this book, please visit:

>   www.keepitgood.org

>   www.lulu.com

ACKNOWLEDGEMENTS

This book would not have been possible without the phenomenal support of an important group of people. First, to my husband, John, thank you for supporting and encouraging me over the nine years of early mornings and weekends that went into writing this book. Thank you to my children, McKenna and Jack, for being a constant source of inspiration. Thank you to Mama, Corey, Richard, and the rest of my family for your constant love and support.

Thank you to Mr. Tom Gilson for providing a critical review and for editing the early versions of this book. Thank you to Ms. Kathleen Poe Ross and Ms. Laura Poe for editing later versions as well.

Thank you, Kevin Queen of 12Stone Church for telling me to "keep pouring out your heart on the keyboard and try not to edit out the fire." Your encouragement meant more to me than you know.

Also, thank you so much to my dear stepsister, Tracy, for helping in the design the cover for this book and helping me through the formatting phase. Please visit Tracy's website at studiocharliecreative. com to see more of her amazing work.

I would like to say a special thank you to Mr. Tri Robinson, author of *Saving God's Green Earth* for performing a critical review of the book and serving as a mentor for me through this process.

Most importantly, though, I would like to offer a prayer of gratitude and praise to my Heavenly Father. Thank You for inspiring the parables through epiphany moments over the past nine years. I give all the glory and praise to You, and I pray that this book helps others see what creation means to You.

Dedication

This book is dedicated to my
children, McKenna and Jack.
May you always find joy and
wonder in God's creation.

Contents

FORWARD

For the creation waits with eager longing for the revealing of the children of God; for the creation was subjected to futility, not of its own will but by the will of the one who subjected it, in hope that the creation itself will be set free from its bondage to decay and will obtain the freedom of the glory of the children of God.
— Romans 8:19-22

What might this "eager longing" sound like?

Imagining a message from one awaiting the children of God

Dear Sir or Madam,

As the president of your fan club, it is incumbent upon me to air the following grievance on behalf of all creatures great and small. Perhaps you didn't know that you had a fan club. We'll get to that.

First, my name is Ruban Quercus. I am a 300-year-old Red Oak Tree located on the front lawn of the church here on Main Street.

Now, before I continue, I must say what a joy it is for me to watch all the believers flock to church each Sunday to worship our Lord and savior Jesus Christ. "*Our?*" you might be asking, "Jesus is *your* savior too?" Oh yes. It is written: "*The hope promised by the gospel has been proclaimed to every creature under heaven"* (Colossians 1:23), which includes me. However, Jesus is my savior in a slightly different way than He is yours.

It all goes back to that infamous day in the Garden. By eating the fruit of the Tree of Knowledge of Good and Evil (or TOK, as we creatures call him), Adam and Eve messed things up for everyone. It was the bite heard 'round the world...

You see, things were so different back then. The fan club numbers are dwindling now, but back then, EVERY creature was Adam and Eve's biggest fans. What a thrill it was to have one of our own — another creature like us — actually made in the image of God! That's why we were so glad when God put Adam in charge in the Garden to "till it and keep it" (Genesis 2:15) and why we were so heartbroken when they ate the forbidden fruit.

It's almost too painful to mention. But I have to say, when she and Adam took those bites and when they dropped that ball ... Let's see, how can I explain this? Okay, imagine the "awwww" you hear in a crowded stadium when a player misses the winning shot in a basketball game and multiply that by a gazillion.

Instead of an arena with a measly 20,000 people groaning in disappointment, imagine a heart-wrenching cry of agonizing disappointment from every bird, every blade of grass, every tree, every fish, every tiny bacterium, and indeed all of creation—for we knew what was in store for us. We were now in bondage (Romans 8:21).

Instantly, our two heroes whom God had given dominion over us, who gave each of us names, had gone from justly watching over us as one of our own to unjustly overseeing us as slave owners. That's one reason God said, "cursed is the ground because of you" (Genesis 3:17), for now we had to put forth thorns and thistles to protect ourselves (hence the mighty groan).

And did I mention that this outcry is ongoing? For thousands of years our collective "awww" has continued constantly because of this curse. Just like Paul observed in Romans 8, "The whole creation has been groaning in labor pains until now." You humans cannot hear our suffering, but some of you, such as Paul, can sense it.

That, ladies and gentlemen, brings me back to the main point of my message. God's Word is crystal clear about His appreciation for and devotion to His creation, yet many Christians are living as if they have never heard of these things. This is the crux of my complaint.

There are some of you out there who recognize the eternal and Biblical value of God's creation and live creation-respectful and glory-giving lives, but it is definitely not all of the Body of Christ. This is why seeing the congregation flocking to church is such a joy for me. I know that means we are one step closer to the freedom from our bondage—the "freedom of the glory of the children of God" (Romans 8).

All that is to say that until the true children of God are revealed, I implore God's people, the body of Christ reading this book, to please be the world leaders God has called you to be for the benefit of His creation and His people. It's so plain in the Bible that God cares for His creation and He wants you to care for us, too.

This book you're holding in your hands was written by a friend of mine who is trying to show Christians what creation means to God and how preserving it can improve the quality of life of everyone on Earth and draw more people to God for His glory.

The pages that follow this message contain the first of eight parables illustrating these points.

It is my prayer that the pieces of the puzzle would become clear to you through the chapters and parables, as they were for Adam and Eve before the Fall, and as they will be when the children of God are revealed when our Lord and Savior brings us all home

Sincerely,

Sir Ruban Quercus III

P.S. You may be wondering how I earned my knighthood. I am a mighty warrior for the Kingdom and was honored with this distinction because of the number of people who have looked at me and thought about God. As the wise King Solomon once said, "*From the greatness and beauty of created things comes a corresponding perception of their Creator*" (Wisdom of Solomon 13:5).

The Tale of the Middle-Aged Geologist (Part One)

"I hear the organ! Come on!!" Three well-dressed friends run down a San Francisco sidewalk toward a church. After a late night on the streets of San Fran, they overslept, took too many wrong turns on the way, circled the block four times to find parking, and now they are late to a friend's wedding. With suit jackets flapping, their dress shoes pound the concrete on the race toward the steps bursting in hydrangeas and white ribbon. One of the three tardy guests, a cousin of the groom, trails behind the others as he attempts to text "Coming in" in response to his mother's "Where are you?!?" message.

As he hits send, it happens: Something catches his foot and he hurtles forward, arms windmilling in a futile attempt to regain balance. The next moment, he is sprawled out on the sidewalk next to his cell phone, now with a badly cracked screen.

Stunned, he looks around for the cause of this inconvenience and sees an old homeless man rubbing one of his legs as he sits there stretched out across the sidewalk. He starts to tell off the ragged old man, but decides not to out of fear that a fellow wedding guest might hear him. He rises to his feet and brushes himself off as his friends (who had not seen him fall) climb the steps to the church. Picking up his cracked phone, the wedding guest apologizes to the homeless man and reaches out his hand to help the old beggar to his feet. As his hand meets the grizzled, calloused skin of the homeless man's hand, they lock eyes.

Immediately the rest of the world melts away. There is something about this man's eyes—fascinating yet horrifying, wise yet regretful, wild yet knowledgeable. The wedding guest is utterly transfixed, as if invisible harpoons had shot out of each of these feral pupils and lodged in the young man's soul. Staring in helpless bewilderment, the wedding guest hears the wildest and most intense voice he has ever heard say,

"There was a plane..."

(To be continued...)

INTRODUCTION

Have you ever noticed that some questions about God are easier to answer than others? From my experience, churches do a pretty good job of answering the question, "Does God care about people?" In case you haven't heard, the answer is a resounding "YES!" God loves us. He loves His children more than we will ever truly understand. But many other questions about Him, especially those regarding non-human concerns, are a little tougher to answer. What does God think of His creation? How do we know? What does He want us to do?

Perhaps the two sets of questions go together. Maybe His creation, His beautiful masterpiece, with its resources and glory-giving grandeur, is one expression of His infinite love for us. But how are we responding to this love?

At the dawn of time, when Adam and Eve were in the Garden, we humans knew how to treat creation. We gave it the respect it deserved and honored all of God's creatures as the "master-pieces" they are. But when sin entered our hearts, it brought along its best buddies: pride, greed, and selfishness. As a result, humans wanted more out of creation: more things, more comfort, more status. Ever since the Fall, creation has kept giving us the "more and more" we demand, but still we are never satisfied. Our expectations and desires just continue to grow, and now we are beginning to see the effects as creation stumbles and sways under the weight of our discontent.

But we convince ourselves that we are doing what's right. We say, "God gave us all things for our enjoyment," and "We're going to get a new heaven and a new earth in the end times, anyway, so who cares about this one?" I've heard both excuses many times. They are usually accompanied with a "you only live once" kind of an attitude. We seem to say, *"Go ahead. Indulge. You deserve it..."* as we rationalize away our destructive self-indulgence and greed. But I don't think that's what God's Word is really saying.

Just as the serpent twisted God's words in the Garden to convince Eve to eat the fruit, and just as the enemy said, "It is written" during Jesus' temptation, Christians have come to accept twisted snippets of incomplete verses about creation as Truth. This book is a humble attempt to demonstrate how God views His creation based on a critical review of key verses throughout the Bible. It contains the efforts of one passionate follower of Christ, fumbling toward righteousness, being led by God to say something that needs to be said.

Each chapter in *Keep it Good* begins with a parable rooted in Biblical principles. The wedding guest racing toward the church at the start of this section is the first part of one that will be completed later. These parables are based on stories from my own life, historical figures, or literature. They came to me over the past nine years as I was going about my daily life: sitting in a faculty meeting, driving down the road, relaxing on the couch, reading a student's paper, and rocking my daughter to sleep. These parables opened my eyes to the scriptures about God's creation in such a powerful way that I knew them to be "God-kindled," to use a term coined by C. S. Lewis. In fact, I almost published this under a pen name because I felt (and still feel) that I could not take credit for the work. Each story-metaphor, or parable, is a spark intended to light up an area of our hearts that has previously been cloaked in darkness and open our minds to God's will for His creation.

I realize this topic may feel like uncharted territory for many readers. If that describes you at the present moment, please know that this book is different from what you might expect. *Keep It Good* is for Christians who love God and want to do His will, but for whom the noise and clamor of the world have drowned out aspects of God's word having to do with creation. Still, since many might suspect ulterior motives, I would like to take a moment to address some common suspicions and explain that this book is NOT:

Political. I know that's what many of you are thinking, but you are wrong. This book is not pushing a legislative agenda. In our tendency to categorize topics as "for Democrats" or "for Republicans," as if they are the pink and blue aisles of the toy store, many Christians have lumped all things having to do with nature with the Democratic agenda. But that is not the purpose of this book. God's creation should transcend politics. I ask you to continue reading as a Christian and a part of God's glorious creation, not as a member of one political party or another. After all, girls can play with blocks and pretend to be engineers. And there's nothing wrong with boys pretending to be chefs in a toy kitchen. There just may be something that you are missing.

Gloom and Doom. Yes, we have some major environmental problems throughout the globe. That fact is irrefutable. But I do not think God wants me to write a another long list of looming environmental catastrophes, demonstrating how we are in the proverbial barrel about to plunge to our imminent demise over the roaring waters of our bad choices. While I think many of such publications are informative, even necessary, from my perspective, they do not seem to be fulfilling the task they set out to pursue. This book is not intended to argue over various scientific models, or educate you on the details of the world's environmental problems. I will even be so bold as to say that this is *not* a depressing book.

A judgmental to-do list. This book is not intended to judge you, make you feel judged, load on the guilt trips, or tell you what to do. I think a different story needs to be told. Besides, I am certainly not perfect in this respect. My ecological footprint is larger than I'd like to admit. If you need to make changes in your life, I believe God will prompt your heart through the parables and scripture in this book as He did mine.

Overly scientific. I wanted this book to speak to the average person's experience and knowledge. The concepts in this book are based, first and foremost, in Biblical principles and only secondly in scientific concepts. I have kept the statistics and scientific jargon to a minimum. In my years as a science teacher, I've learned how too much "science-ese" can cause the average joe's mind to "go on screensaver," as my husband says. I want the message of this book to speak to the heart, not just the analytical mind.

Suggesting we all become Amish. Although I admire the way Amish people live, and I believe they show extraordinary wisdom in their choices, I realize that it would not be possible for all of humanity to do away with all forms of pollution and live in perfect harmony with nature. Still, I believe that many of the environmental problems we face can be changed with a simple change in our outlook toward God's creation.

To illustrate these four points, allow me to give this one example: Contrary to every other book I've seen on this topic, you will not see the words global warming or climate change anywhere in this book other than this sentence. Let's save those conversations for another time. Right now, we are going to focus on God's holy and perfect Word and what it means for us, right here and now.

Now that we're clear on what *Keep it Good* is not, the purpose of this book is to show Christians how too many of us are missing the mark when it comes to God's creation. We must understand the disconnect between our actions toward creation and God's intended purpose for creation. Correcting our outlook will enable us to make scripture-informed choices regarding God's creation that glorify God and spread His gospel. In other words, I have felt called to write this, not in finger-pointing judgment of Christianity, but as an extended hand inviting the Body of Christ to come up a little higher.

More specifically, this book seeks to address the following questions:

How does God view His creation?
How do we act toward God's creation?
How should we view His creation?
Didn't God give us all things for our enjoyment?
Why should we bother if we're getting a new heaven and earth anyway?

Introduction

What is the Biblical value of creation?
How does creation destruction hurt "the least of these?"
Where should we go from here?

I address these questions over the course of seven chapters, each with a central parable, or metaphor, rooted in critical verses of the Bible.

Chapter 1 demonstrates God's heart toward His creation, as we understand it from scripture. Although people are first in God's heart, God also cares deeply for the rest of His creation and "has His eye on the sparrow" (Matthew 6), "visits the earth to water it" (Psalm 65), and watches over every little detail such as "when the mountain goat gives birth" (Job 39). Chapter 2 examines our interpretation of God's blessings in the Garden and other verses as excuses to live greedy, creation-abusive lives. The Apostle Paul's description of creation's "bondage to decay" in Romans 8 is the focus of Chapter 3, and how God wants us to change our tune to sing a new song. Chapter 4 details the immense biblical value God's creation has for His children. Chapter 5 discusses how creation preservation is an effective way to care for the "least" Jesus describes in Matthew 25. In Chapter 6, I challenge the reader to examine his or her mentality (or mine-tality), and to consider how trusting God and living according to the Bible would solve most of our problems in creation. Finally, Chapter 7 addresses how we can move forward and break the bonds of our creation-abusive addiction.

Honestly, there is really nothing in this book that has not already been said in one way or another by others who are much smarter than I. This book is just a fresh take on an ancient notion—a notion that used to be very clear to us when we were working the land and living in close fellowship with His creation. But one technological advance after another moves us farther and farther away from creation, and now we've lost touch with that which was once so obvious.

My background and experiences have granted me a unique perspective on these issues, but I am admittedly not an expert. I am not a theologian or an environmental scientist. I am a university teacher who is just trying to follow the will of God in her life. In this sense, I feel somewhat of a connection to C. S. Lewis—not in comparison to his writing (he was a literary genius) but in terms of our professional situations and life-callings as laymen trying to say things that need to be said.

To sum up the whole book in one phrase, I firmly believe that God's word is clear: **You can't be pro-God and anti-creation.** What do I mean by this? Just ask yourself one question: How would you want *your* children to treat *your* creation? I realize your first reaction to that statement might be "Well, I'm not anti-creation." But what if I were to substitute the word "environment" for the word creation? Since many Christians seem to place all things "environmental" (creation) on the liberal aisle of the political toy store, they believe their creation-destructive lifestyles are justified. I would like to help you *imagine* a different possibility through the chapters' parables. And to begin this journey of the imagination, I'd like you to do me a favor…

Over the years of reading God's Word in my own quiet time, a list of verses has helped open my eyes to God's views of creation. There are hundreds of similar verses in the Bible, but only certain ones seem to scream "critical." I'd like to ask you to read these verses. Get your Bible out, read the passages in order, pray about them, and reflect on what you learn in the process. If you're highly skeptical about the subject of creation-care, it's doubly important for you to do this. Even if you are an accomplished Bible student and have many of these passages memorized, please humor me and read them in their entirety. If possible, consider reading outdoors in God's creation— somewhere away from human structures and sounds. After reading, reflect on the verses' meaning and ask God for clarity about what His creation means to Him and what we are to do about it.

Introduction

My Prayer for this Book

God, I pray that this book will show Your children how You feel about Your creation. Speak to their hearts, God, if You want them to make changes, whatever they may be. I pray this book would not be depressing, but enlightening. I do not want the reader to feel judged or accused, but informed and empowered. If You want them to make changes, prompt their hearts and show me how to help. In Jesus' mighty name.

Critical Verses

God's view of His of creation:

Psalm 24:1-2

Psalm 104

Romans 1:20

Genesis 1:31, 2:15, 8:20-9:17

Human action in creation:

Genesis 3:17-19

Job 28, 39, & 40

Romans 8:19-23

Isaiah 24:4-5

Revelation 11:18

Now let's get started.

PART ONE

HOW WE'RE MISSING THE MARK

There's no place like home...

"Just 24 more payments, Evie!" Walter Jones announces to his wife, Evelyn, as he leaves the bedroom one morning in his navy blue fleece bathrobe. Such an announcement is a little monthly tradition for Walter now. When the mortgage bill comes in the mail, he sits down at his desk, writes the check, and puts it in the envelope. Then he picks up a red sharpie and turns to a piece of printer paper taped to the wall. Filling up the page in bold, black font, each number from 100 to 0 stands in line, waiting for its turn to receive a red X through its center. So far, all numbers 25 and higher had received this honor, and yesterday he crossed off number 24.

Now, with his Ziggy coffee cup in one hand and the momentous bill in the other, he marches out the front door, taking care to close the screen door behind him so the cat doesn't get out, and heads for the mailbox. After raising its flag, he pauses at the end of his driveway. Looking back at his home, he takes a moment to reflect on the last decade.

***

Getting to this point in life had not been easy for them. Up until ten years ago, financial hardships were a daily concern. Walter was the only son of a single mom who had to work two jobs to keep food on the table. Evelyn was the daughter of an immigrant family whose parents struggled to get on their feet in a new country. Both Walter and Evelyn were the first in their families to go to college, where they met and fell in love. After graduating with their degrees, Walter's in finance and Evelyn's in nursing, they eloped at the courthouse and started a life together in Walter's one-bedroom apartment.

After a few years, Walter came home from work and announced that he had found their dream home. When Evelyn first laid eyes on the fixer-upper (to put it nicely) she was very apprehensive. Still, it was a steal in a great neighborhood, so they invested their life savings in a down payment and became homeowners.

The running joke that first year was that they were George and Mary Bailey from *It's a Wonderful Life* living in that run-down old house with broken windows. Like the Baileys, they knew exactly where to position buckets, saucepans, empty garbage cans, and any other kind of container they could get their hands on whenever the forecast called for showers. But after months of saving every penny they could, they slowly started patching up holes, ripping up carpets, painting the walls, and furnishing their home.

Once the house was becoming more livable, they moved on to the yard. "The jungle," as Walter called the front lawn, was completely overgrown when they first moved in. Weeks of sweat-drenched manual labor went by before they could get the yard back to a presentable state. But they found that they really enjoyed working outdoors together and yard work became a part of their Saturday morning routine. Now, beautifully landscaped grounds with flowerbeds, vegetable gardens, and outdoor light fixtures surround their house.

On one of those Saturday mornings in the garden, as Evelyn reached for the next clump of weeds, she asked, "What do you think about getting a pet or two?" Growing up, neither of their families was able to afford a pet, but they always liked the idea and decided to give it a try. Still, having solittle experience, they decided to start with a parakeet, which they named Mr. Chirpmaster, and a goldfish, Hank. After successfully keeping them alive for a full six months, they expanded their little family further at the local animal shelter with their sweet dog, Murphy, and their rambunctious cat, Patches. Murphy and Patches were the babies of the house, and the Joneses were their doting parents.

Murphy and Patches brought tremendous joy to the Joneses, but there was still something missing. They loved working the land and playing with their pets, but they still longed to experience it all with others with whom they could have an even deeper relationship: ones they could really share their hearts with, teach right from wrong, and show how to care for their land the way they did.

Nine months after this realization, little William Jones was born, followed by Allison a year later. Unique and wonderful, they were like mirror images of Walter and Evelyn. The couple loved their children beyond what words could say. Still, they remained faithful to their other commitments. They fixed leaky pipes, pulled up weeds out of the lawn, grew vegetables to nourish their family, and continued to care for Murphy, Patches, Mr. Chirpmaster, and Hank III with tender devotion.

***

Walter takes a deep breath. Now, 10 years after purchasing their fixer-upper, with only 24 more mortgage payments to go, Walter stands at the end of his driveway looking out on the home that he and his wife built. This is more than just a place where he can hang his hat. This is a place that brings joy and satisfaction through their hard work. This is a place where he can be himself and share his heart. And most of all, this is a place that provides a safe and nurturing home for his children to play, grow, and learn. As Walter stands there reflecting on all these things, he thinks to himself, "indeed, it all was very good.

CHAPTER ONE

Home

God enjoys and cares for His creation

Homes of all shapes and sizes protect us from the elements, allow us to put down roots in a community, and give us a nurturing place to raise our children. What did you feel while you pictured the parable on the previous pages? Happiness? Contentment? Satisfaction? Or maybe longing? Nostalgia? Perhaps you envisioned yourself standing in your current home or maybe the home of your childhood. Take a moment to reflect.

If you have children, it was probably easy for you to empathize with the Joneses' desire to provide a nurturing home for William and Allison. I expect that you also understood their dedication to the preservation of their home as well. If you have a home like the one described above, you probably do many of the same things to foster a healthy living environment for you and your family. Perhaps you mow the grass every weekend, fix leaky sinks, and take care of beloved pets, among other tasks. As it does for Walter and Evelyn, reflecting on these things may bring contentment, satisfaction, and gratitude for the multitude of blessings God has bestowed upon you. Through your physical and mental gifts and by guiding your circumstances just right, God has blessed you with the ability to establish your little world—your home, your "creation." It is, in a sense, a statement about your hard work: a place to nurture your family, something to help your children in the future, and, by extension, a physical expression of your love. Surely all parents want to give their children a home like this, where they can just enjoy life and learn valuable lessons about respect, hard work, and love.

***

Now, how do you think *God* sees *His* creation? *His* animals? *His* plants? *His* Earth? Is it possible that God views His creation even a little bit like the way we view ours? Obviously, He loves us, His children, above all else and would sacrifice anything for us. But does that mean He does not care for the rest of His creation *at all?*

Since we are made in the image of God, I believe we can get hints about His heart toward His creation by examining our own.

Snapshots of God

I've always loved scrapbooks. Scrapbooks (or, more commonly nowadays, Facebook photo albums) reveal people's passions, interests, and life experiences. If you've never met a person before, and if you've never heard stories from others about her, you could get a pretty good sense about her by checking out her Facebook albums. However, while the images and mementos kept in scrapbooks give us a better understanding of a person, they are not the whole story.

As we see in Genesis 1:26, humankind was made in the image of God: *"Then God said, 'Let us make humankind in our image, according to our likeness.'"* Just like photos in an album, we are not exact clones, but we are a glimpse or a flash of Him. Compared to God, we are simple, two-dimensional snapshots of God's multi-dimensional magnificence. Still, despite our simplicity, we *can* get a sense of God's heart by examining the good, loving, and righteous aspects of humanity.

From the creation of light until the dawn of humanity, God's mighty words caused the entire universe to come into being. The fullness of this power and grandeur we will never truly understand. But even though we don't know what it is like to create the universe, we *do* know what it is like to create a home and a life for our children. In that sense, I think God sowed little hints about His heart toward His creation into us as He formed us in His image—His little scrapbook, of Himself.

While our creations are miniscule compared to God's masterpiece, I believe we *can* learn something about God's heart toward creation by looking at the relationship between people and their homes. After all, these mini-creations are of paramount importance to us, so much so that we celebrate each step of the process: buying that fixer-upper, cleaning up the yard, having our children, and more. In the introductory analogy, you may have picked up on these small celebrations as Walter reflected on their accomplishments. Looking out at his house, he thought back fondly to fixing the leaky roof, time spent in the yard, and the whole process. Each step in the "creation" of his little world was "good" in his eyes.

Walter Jones stood in his driveway enjoying the fruits of his labor, and in a sense, I believe God did the same at the time of creation. Why else would He go through the trouble of saying that each step of the way was "good"? I mean, of course it was good. God, the author of all love and righteousness, cannot create anything that is *bad*, so being good goes without saying. Still, God took the trouble to tell all of humanity that every step of the way in His work forming creation was good.

Think about it: The same voice that spoke all of the universe into being took a moment after each step in creation and also said, "It is good." Nowhere else in the Bible is God so specific and repetitive about His praises in this way. The significance of this seemingly simple step cannot be overstated.

But *how* was it good? The word "good" is thrown around so much in our society that it has lost much of its meaning. A simple Google search of "good" yields over 11 million results with responses ranging from "good restaurant" to "good dog." What does good mean to God, exactly?

One way to understand that question is to look at what He *didn't* say. For example, He didn't say, "It is done," or finished, or complete, as if to say, "OK, let's move on to the next thing on my checklist." No, He stepped back and admired His work at each point. Also, He didn't say, "It is *incomplete*." Our omnipotent God knew He still had five more days of creation to go after making light, but despite the work He still had before Him, God didn't seem to focus on how much farther He had left to go. Finally, on the sixth day, after creating all of the heavens and the Earth, God *didn't* say, "It is done." As if to say, "Boy, I'm glad that's over! Humanity, this is your problem now," as if we were expected to make the clouds rain and have *our* eyes on the sparrows.

No, the creator of the universe looked out on everything His hands had made and said, "indeed it is very good," like a contractor examining a job well done, a teacher watching students graduate, or a doctor watching a previously sick patient leave the hospital. Just like Walter and Evelyn got joy and satisfaction from each step of their lives (buying the house, fixing it up, adopting pets) I believe God called each step good because He felt similar joy and satisfaction. As "Wisdom" personified says in Proverbs 8:30-31, "*...when He marked out the foundations of the earth, then I was beside him, like a master worker; and I was daily his delight, rejoicing before him always, rejoicing in His inhabited world and delighting in the human race.*"

God's Word on His Creation

While reflecting on our own "creations" is helpful, our personal experiences as two-dimensional snapshots of God's heart aren't the only evidence of His devotion to creation. After all, while looking though a scrapbook gives you a clue about someone, reading his or her journal or other personal writings can tell you even more. The Bible, God's written Word, is His instruction manual for life and His letters of love and adoration for His children, all rolled into one. When Christians have questions about how God feels on a subject, they should turn to His Word for the answers. So what does the Bible say about God's heart toward His creation?

Many verses throughout the Bible show how God takes personal ownership of creation — and God is not a hands-off kind of owner, either. Consider the following verses:

- *For every wild animal of the forest is mine, the cattle on a thousand hills. I know all the birds of the air, and all that moves in the field is mine.* — Psalm 50:10-11
- *The Earth and its fullness are the Lord's.* — Corinthians 10:26
- *The earth is the Lord's and all that is in it, the world, and those who live in it; for he has founded it on the seas, and established it on the rivers.* — Psalm 24:1-2
- *You visit the earth and water it, you greatly enrich it ... The pastures of the wilderness overflow, the hills gird themselves with joy, the meadows clothe themselves with flocks, the valleys deck themselves with grain, they shout and sing together for joy.* —Psalm 65:9-13
- *Your righteousness is like the mighty mountains, your judgments are like the great deep; you save humans and animals alike, O Lord.* — Psalm 36:6
- *You make springs gush forth in the valleys, they flow between the hills, giving water to every wild animal ... the earth is satisfied from the fruit of your work.* — Psalm 104:10-13
- [All creatures look to God] *"to give them their food in due season; when you give to them, they gather it up; when you open your hand, they are filled with good things.* — Psalm 104:27-28

Or as our Lord and Savior, Jesus, explained: *"Are not two sparrows sold for a penny? Yet not one of them will fall to the ground apart from your Father"* (Matthew 10:29). Amazingly, God cares for every tiny, seemingly insignificant creature, and the book of Job reveals one of the clearest examples of God's level of care and attention to His creation.

First, let me give you a little context. Other than Jesus, no one else in the Bible suffered more than Job. In a very short period of time, Job lost his wealth, his entire family, and even his health. In the chapters leading up to chapters 38 and 39, Job challenges God, telling Him he did not deserve to have all these bad things happen to him. God responds with incredibly detailed examples of His care of creation, to demonstrate that the all-powerful, all-knowing, and all-seeing creator knows what He is doing in Job's life. Little Job—in his limited wisdom and narrow view of the world—does not.

Starting at the dawn of creation, God explains how He laid the Earth's foundations and determined the boundaries of the seas, commands the morning to expose light to the darkness, and keeps a record of various natural resources as He walks in the recesses of the deep and sees the storehouses of snow.

God asks Job a series of questions to put Job in his place:

> *Where were you when I laid the foundation of the earth? Tell me, if you have understanding. Who determined its measurements—surely you know! ... Have you entered the storehouses of the snow, or have you seen the storehouses of the hail, which I have reserved for the time of trouble, for the day of battle and war? ... Who has cut a channel for the torrents of rain, and a way for the thunderbolt, to bring rain on a land where no one lives, on the desert, which is empty of human life, to satisfy the waste and desolate land, and to make the ground put forth grass? ... Who has the wisdom to number the clouds? Or who can tilt the waterskins of the heavens...*
> —Job 38:4-37.

His attention toward His loving creatures is even more detailed. God feeds the lion cubs, provides for the raven, and knows the instant any of His creatures give birth. He helps the young become strong so they can go out from their mothers and continue spreading the species. He knows exactly how many days each and every creature on the face of the Earth lives:

> *Can you hunt the prey for the lion, or satisfy the appetite of the young lions, when they couch in their dens, or lie in wait in their covert? Who provides for the raven its prey, when its young ones cry to God, and wander about for lack of food? Do you know when the mountain goat gives birth? Do you observe the calving of the deer? Can you number the months that they*

fulfill, and do you know the time when they give birth, when they crouch to give birth to their offspring, and are delivered of their young? —Job 38:39-39:3

The breadth of the level of care God reveals here is difficult to take in. Scientists estimate there are between 7 and 9 million different species on the planet. At any moment throughout all of time, God knew the exact number of clouds in the sky; He sent every lightning bolt to its place; watched every baby creature being born; fed every creature in turn; and kept a record of each of their lives. That level of detail is absolutely mind-boggling.

When I think of this, the story of Noah becomes a little clearer. God commanded Noah to build the ark because mankind was corrupt and filled with violence. His precious animals were innocent, though, so He wanted them to continue on in the new world:

And of every living thing, of all flesh, you shall bring two of every kind into the ark, to keep them alive with you; they shall be male and female. Of the birds according to their kinds, and of the animals according to their kinds, of every creeping thing of the ground according to its kind, two of every kind shall come in to you, to keep them alive. — Genesis 6:19-20

After the flood, God made a covenant with Noah and every living creature that He would never again destroy them all by water. Like the Noah story, there are many other examples of God "*saving humans and animals alike*" (Psalm 36:6), which amaze or baffle scientists today (and the rest of us too).

Examples of God's Care of Creation in Nature

Ever since I was a middle school summer camper, I loved learning about God's creation. Hiking in the mountains of North Carolina, finding the glow-in-the-dark fungus among rotting wood, feeling the icy cold spring-fed water in a search for salamanders, smelling the cherry-scented centipedes, tasting the wild mountain blueberries, and even hearing the alarmingly loud rattle of the Eastern Diamondback from a crack in the bald rock of the mountain: It was all so fascinating to me. I carried this love of the natural world through high school and college and decided to become a science teacher because of it.

Looking back, I see my fascination in a new light. Scientific understanding of the natural world gave me a glimpse of the almighty power and wisdom of God. A close look at any organism in any ecosystem across the biosphere shows that each creature has a specific role to play in its little habitat, and everything about its physical and behavioral adaptations make it uniquely fitted to do that exact job. Many times the adaptations make logical sense. Other times, however, they are absolutely astounding. Sea turtles, for example, are able to find the exact beach where they were born after traveling thousands of miles across all the oceans of the world. I can hardly find my car in the parking lot, and I certainly don't remember anything before age four!

The giant redwoods of California breathe the same air Jesus breathed: many of them were alive 2,000 years ago. They have survived mudslides, fires, storms, and anything else nature could throw their way. Even God's tiniest creatures are amazing. There is a caterpillar in the frozen tundra that lives for decades and has the natural equivalent of antifreeze in its blood. Every winter, the caterpillar hibernates until it is warm enough to continue feeding. It takes this caterpillar *years* to become a butterfly.

Why would God put antifreeze in this amazing creature's blood? Why would He bother creating something that is such an exception to every natural rule, every bit of common sense?

To parallel this example, allow me to tell you a story. My husband, John, and I took our honeymoon on the island of St. Lucia in the Caribbean. Of the many wonderful experiences we had in that island paradise, one thing that stands out in our minds is a tour of the active volcano known as La Soufriere. As we stood in the tour group hearing about the massive power below the surface of those muddy, bubbling sulfur pits, one of the nervous guests asked the tour guide about the chances of the volcano erupting. After reassuring us that it had been dormant for thousands of years, the guide explained his perspective on the possibility of the volcano's eruption in this way:

> I'm not worried about the volcano erupting today. You know why? Listen: The birds sing in the trees. The insects buzz around everywhere. Animals scurry along on the forest floor. Life goes on as usual. Now, if those things *weren't* happening, and if it was completely silent, *then* I'd be running for my life! Animals can sense when major natural events are about to take place. Look at the recent tsunami in Indonesia. There were elephants that were chained to the beach, and they broke their chains and ran to higher ground even *before* the waters receded back from the beach and long before anyone could see the massive wave. There were other stories of goldfish jumping out of their bowls or pets acting very strangely before that event. Keep that in mind. So, if we are going along on this tour, and you stop hearing the sounds of nature, and you see birds of all different species flying in the same direction, follow them. I know I will! They know something you don't.

This story piqued my interest, so I did more research. From Pompeii to the recent earthquake and tsunami in Japan, stories of animals acting strangely prior to natural disasters accompanied every major event I could find. For example, Professor Helmut Tributsch stated in his fascinating book, *When Snakes Awake - Animals and Earthquake Prediction* (MIT Press, 1984)[1], "Two days before an earthquake struck Helice, Greece, in 373 B.C., the snakes, weasels, and worms deserted the city. Minutes before the Naples quake of 1805, oxen, sheep, dogs, and geese cried out in unison. A herd of horses tore loose and ran off in panic just prior to the San Francisco earthquake of 1906 ..."

But what's even more interesting is that scientists have no idea why this occurs, or *how* all animals can do this. The DNA of a goldfish is

[1]"Overview, When Snakes Awake: Animals and Earthquake Prediction by Helmut Tributsch", MIT Press, 2016,

vastly different from that of an elephant. How could these creatures exhibit similar behavioral traits? How could all the different species of birds know which direction to fly away from a volcano? How could different animals know to desert a city prior to an earthquake? Scientists can't figure it out. The only answer is God. God truly cares for His creation in ways we will never fully understand and goes through great effort to preserve it.

Why Does God Care?

That leads me to my next question: Why does God care about creation? Why would God go through the trouble? Keeping an exact tally of the number of clouds in the sky seems daunting. To shed a little light on this concept, let's take a look at football (go with me here).

I never liked football growing up. Both of my parents loved the game, but I couldn't have cared less about it. It seemed like football was always on TV, but I would just tune it out. It was just noise on the screen out there in the other room. However, when I went to college and got to know some of the individual players, I started to feel a connection to the game. They were students just like me. I knew their names. I knew their majors. They weren't just *numbers* running around out there, they were Aaron, Kwame, David, and the others. I couldn't miss a game. I screamed at the television screen after big plays. When I would see one of them hurt on the field, I would be intensely concerned for them, praying to God that they would get up, breathing a heavy sigh of relief when they rose to their feet. I encouraged them when I saw them on their crutches in the halls or in class. I wished I could do more to help their recovery. I was connected. I was invested personally.

It may sound strange, but I think this analogy can help us understand why God cares so deeply for His creation. Take birds, for example. To a passive observer, birds in a forest may just be squawking, noisy things that drop white splotches on your windshield. However, if you know the birds—their names, which trees they build their nests in, what they eat, what their songs sound like—you become personally invested. It isn't just tweeting and squawking in the tree outside your window anymore. It's a cardinal, a Carolina chickadee, a brown thrasher. You find yourself putting up a bird feeder to see more of them. You look forward to the summer and a visit from the majestic ruby-throated hummingbird. They're almost like friends. You begin to cheer them on, and you want to fight for them.

So when you find out, for example, that the red-cockaded woodpecker is at risk of extinction due to the destruction of the only habitat where these birds can survive (old-growth long-leaf pine forests) you get angry. Couldn't they build their shopping mall somewhere else? That's the only place this masterpiece, this perfect creature of God's can survive! Who are we to wipe out one of God's creations? Do we think we know better than He does?

I observed this paradigm shift while doing my dissertation work in Hawaii alongside fellow educators. When teachers go out snorkeling with little or no prior knowledge about tropical fish, they'll have a pretty good time but be out of the water within 15 minutes. However, if you put a waterproof fish-identification card in their hands with an underwater pencil, they begin to identify fish by name. They start collecting them. They stay in the water much longer and come out saying, "Did you see that Moorish idol?" "No! I'm so jealous!" They look up species in their identification books to find out more about them. Looking back on her experiences with Hawaiian wildlife, one participant had this to say:

> I have to be honest. I wasn't excited about learning about reef fish at all. Fish have never really been my thing. Before now, they all just kinda looked the same to me ... Big one, small one, black one, yellow one, stripey one, etcetera, etcetera.
> Today was a full day of snorkeling and fish observations. I went into it thinking I would just have to endure it, but by the end of the day, I was so into it!

When asked if one event or activity from Hawaii stood out in her memory, this participant said, "By far it was the fish. I loved that. I love being able to tell the difference between a Moorish idol and a pennant tang." Through this direct experience with these majestic creatures, the teachers became personally invested, which made their reaction to the news of ocean pollution change.

When the native Hawaiians began telling the teachers about the reef being at risk, the teachers wanted to know what was being done to protect the fish. They became angry about the marine pollution. They were shocked to hear that a Los Angeles Police Department road barrier floated thousands of miles across the ocean to end up on a Hawaiian beach. The Hawaiians asked us if we could schedule time in our jam-packed itinerary to clean up beach litter. And some of these teachers didn't even recycle prior to the trip!

This all begs the question: If people can become so personally invested after learning a few species' names and something about their lives, how much more invested is God? The one who knows the exact moment each of them comes into the world, the one who feeds them, protects them, shelters them, the one who created them—it's no wonder He claims *"the earth and all its fullness"* so specifically as "His."

In other words, the answer to "Why does God care?" can be understood in five ways:

It is His. He made it, so it is good.

He enjoys and is blessed by His works. The beauty and grandeur of His hard work brings Him glory (more on this in Chapter 4).

He wants to bless us. Just as the loving home was nurturing to Allison and William, God's creation is intended to nurture and bless us.

God loves life. He has given ALL of His creatures almost supernatural abilities or adaptations that make them perfectly

46

suited for their particular habitat.
But most of all…

God keeps His promises. At the end of the animals' creation, God blessed the creatures and told them to "be fruitful and multiply." Also, after the flood, He promised Noah and every creature that they would never again be totally destroyed by water.

Earlier I asked: "Have you ever noticed that some questions about God are easier to answer than others?" Questions having to do with people exclusively are a little easier ("Thou shall not murder," for example). But questions having to do with humans and natural resources or other organisms are trickier. Stories like that of Walter and Evelyn Jones are attempts to help us imagine aspects of God's heart that might not be crystal clear in the Bible: His love for life, His desire to bless His children, and His care for creation. That deep sense of Truth is ingrained in us as God's scrapbook of Himself. Looking at how we view our own little creations can give us a hint at how God might view His. Like Walter and Evelyn are committed to mowing the lawn or taking the dog to the vet, God is committed to His creation. But just looking at the scrapbook won't tell the whole story. We must also look for evidence in God's word about these things, such as those verses mentioned earlier and look for evidence in the natural world (the animals' amazing survival adaptations and their knowledge of natural disasters before they happen).

God's creation is glorious, God is blessed by His works, God uses creation to bless us, God loves life, and God keeps His promises to humans and creatures. The next chapter will discuss how many of us miss these aspects of God, and become confused as to what our role in creation is supposed to be. After all, how would you want *your* children to treat *your* creation?

"You Only Live Once..."

Back to the Jones family. Fast-forward eleven years...

Allison and William are getting older. In fact, they're about to graduate from high school and are growing more and more independent. Walter and Evelyn are so proud of their children's academic and athletic accomplishments and their ambitions for the future.

Still, like all children (and especially teenagers), they make mistakes sometimes. Walter and Evelyn do their best to steer them in the right direction, but they worry that a few of their kids' friends may be bad influences on them.

One day, Walter and Evelyn announce that they will need to go out of town on a business trip. They consider asking the nice old lady down the street to watch Allison and William, but the two teenagers convince their parents that they are old enough to stay by themselves. Reluctantly, Walter and Evelyn say, "OK, we will be back in a few days. We love you. Enjoy yourselves." The drooping faces of Murphy and Patches peer out of the front window as Walter and Evelyn pack up the car.

As soon as the car is out of sight, the cell phones come out. Those "questionable friends" are the first to receive the news: "Hey, our parents are out of town for the weekend. Why don't you come over for little get-together?" Calls lead to other calls and so on until the "little get-together" has become a full-blown party. A wild party. In fact, the word "party" is too tame to describe the rager that occurs at the Jones household.

By 1 o'clock in the morning, over 150 people are on the Joneses' property. As the night wears on, the debacle escalates: drinking games played at the dining room table, cigarettes smoked inside the house, spinning car tires tearing up the lawn, foaming beer spilled on floors and furniture, dancing party-goers on the coffee table, toilet paper dangling in the trees, and on and on. Through the stupor of their drunkenness, swept away by the illusion of fulfillment, Allison and William turn to each other and say, "Well, they told us to enjoy ourselves!"

***

At 7:30 the next morning, gentle rays of sunlight shine through the big front window of the Jones house and onto William's face on the living room couch, where he had passed out the night before. William lies there with his eyes closed as his mind gradually comes into focus. The first thing he notices (other than the pounding headache) is the smell of stale cigarette smoke and beer. That's strange, he thinks initially, until...

His eyes fly open as reality sets in, and he darts upright. Among all the "friends" passed out on the floor, there isn't a single square foot that does not have a red plastic cup, cigarette butt, piece of a broken coffee table, or some sort of stain. With anxiety setting in, he stands up to look for his sister.

He finds her in the kitchen trying to sweep a line of ants out the back door, which someone had left wide open all night. As she explains this to her brother, William interrupts, "Wait, was this door open when you came down this morning?? Where are Murphy and Patches?"

They search the house and find Murphy cowering under a bed, but Patches and Mr. Chirpmaster are nowhere to be seen, and Hank XIV is belly up next to a beer can. Rushing back downstairs and calling for Patches, Allison and William step outside the back door to find the yard in a similar state of decimation. A sickly sweet smell greets them at their exit, and they turn to see Walter's raised vegetable garden browning under a party-goer's stomach acid. They step farther out into the yard to see if Patches is in the trees or on the roof, and William notices something white on the shingles waving around in the breeze. They know what it is instantly.

With panic mounting, they step over the plastic cups, cigarette butts, and food debris as they run around to the front of the house. Like the thick vines adorning a rainforest, toilet paper drapes every inch of the beautiful trees in front of their house. The only thing parting the way through the TP jungle is a set of tire tracks cutting a deep path through the fescue, into a bordering flower bed, next to a knocked down mailbox, and out onto the road.

Overwhelmed by reality, Allison fights off tears as William grips the hair on the sides of his head. They didn't mean for it to get this bad. They just wanted to have some friends over. They didn't know it would turn into a destructive fiasco. Instead of cutting the party short when things were getting out of hand, William and Allison had gotten caught up in " enjoying themselves." Sure, they could pick up the plastic cups off the ground, but there was no way to undo much of the other damage. With hands trembling, William turns to Allison and asks, "What are Mom and Dad going to say?"

CHAPTER TWO

The Party

How would you want your children to treat your creation?

We've all heard stories of teenage destruction like this. Maybe a movie or TV show came to mind when you read that story. Personally, I cannot watch those programs. Even when a trailer for one comes on TV, I have to look away as I think, *How incredibly disrespectful of their parents, the ones who worked hard for the things the children treated as worthless, the* rightful *owners of the property, the ones who put these teenagers in charge.*

Think back to our earlier picture of Walter Jones standing in his driveway, cup of coffee in hand, reaping the satisfaction and rewards of his hard work. What would he and Mrs. Jones have said if they had come home unexpectedly and walked in on this scene? If this were your home, your creation, what do you think would come to your mind? And in the midst of that, if Allison were to say to you, "Well, you told us to enjoy ourselves," what might *your* reaction be?

In the last chapter, you read scriptures showing God's view of His creation: *It is good... Everything is mine... Every bird of the air is mine... Not one falls to the ground apart from the Father...* Obviously, God is very proud of His creation, watches over every minute detail, and puts a tremendous amount of time and effort into maintaining it. But the story does not end there, unfortunately.

Although God is the founder, CEO, and sole shareholder of creation, He put humanity in charge of general management ("tilling and keeping" the Garden). Also, God blesses us richly and wants us to enjoy all things (1 Timothy 6:17). But would what we're doing be classified as enjoying? Would "exploitation" be a better word to describe much of what we do with God's creation?

This chapter will challenge common assumptions about our blessing in the Garden and our purpose in God's creation, and demonstrate how we disrespect God by abusing our authority in the earth.

Divine Promotion and Free Will

We all love success stories. They make for great entertainment: Frodo destroying the Ring of Power, or Katniss Everdeen wining the Hunger Games. We love hearing inspirational stories of people stepping up to the plate and overcoming great trials. The Bible is chock-full of them. When God assigned tasks to Noah, Moses, Abraham, David, Peter, and others, many (if not all) of them struggled with doubt and maybe even wanted to quit somewhere along their journeys. But they didn't. They overcame their adversities and made it into the "Faith Hall of Fame," so to speak. They doubted themselves, but God knew they were best equipped for the task at hand, so He selected them for *divine promotion.*

Because we are made in the image of God, we are best equipped out of all of God's creatures for the divine promotion of managing God's creatures. It would not make sense for Walter and Evelyn to put Murphy or Patches in charge. Allison and William would be the logical choice. But if we are best suited for this important task, then why do we have so many environmental problems? If a truly God-imaged figure were in charge—someone at least somewhat similar to the author and creator of the universe—then surely he or she would know how to care for and respect this glorious creation, right? The problem arises because of another aspect of our creation: our *free will.*

Instead of making us puppets under His complete control, God gave us free will. A helpful way to understand this challenging concept is to think of the difference between a toy dog and a real dog. Sure a toy dog is nice, and you can get enjoyment out of it. But the level of joy and satisfaction you get from a real dog—one that is fully and completely devoted to you, shows you unconditional love, explodes with excitement every time you walk through the door—*that* kind of affection makes the toy dog look trivial. However, this free will in the hands of imperfect people can be dangerous. Let's be honest, we didn't make it very long before goofing it up. When Adam and Eve ate of the forbidden fruit, they freely chose to disobey God. This choice resulted in expulsion from the garden, separation from God, and a variety of other tragic consequences, two of which affect our behavior toward creation.

First, due to our separation from God, the voice of God is not as clear to us as it was in the Garden. Psalm 19 describes this unheard voice:

> *The heavens are telling the glory of God; and the firmament proclaims his handiwork. Day to day pours forth speech, and night to night declares knowledge. There is no speech, nor are there words; their voice is not heard; yet their voice goes out through all the earth, and their words to the end of the world.* — Psalm 19:1-4a

God's voice is everywhere—in every aspect of creation. Yet there is no speech, nor are there words, so their voice is not heard by humans. I believe the rest of creation that does not have free will *can* still hear this voice. We can observe evidence in the stories from Chapter 1. Animals act strangely before natural disasters as if God was telling them where to go for safety as He tells the sparrow where to find food, and setting the wild donkey free.

Don't get me wrong: We can (and do) still hear His voice, but it is not automatic anymore. Like a rock band drowning out the voice of the person next to us at a concert, our choice to eat of forbidden fruit introduced a lot of noise into our lives. In order to hear God's voice again, we have to pay attention, give God time, and seek His voice through the noise. All too frequently, though, we focus on the noise instead.

This leads me to the second consequence. I've heard people ask, if God's eye is on the sparrow, why doesn't He steer the elephants away from the poachers or stop the bulldozers from tearing down the rainforest? This is the consequence of the fourth curse at the Fall in Genesis. "Four?" you might ask? We normally only focus on the three given to Adam, Eve, and the serpent, but a fourth curse was declared in Genesis 3:17:

> *And to the man he said, "Because you have listened to the voice of your wife, and have eaten of the tree about which I commanded you, 'You shall not eat of it,' cursed is the ground because of you; in toil you shall eat of it all the days of your life; thorns and thistles it shall bring forth for you; and you shall eat the plants of the field. By the sweat of your face you shall eat bread until you return to the ground, for out of it you were taken; you are dust, and to dust you shall return.*

We interpret this verse strictly as a punishment upon us: we sinned, so now we have to labor for our food. While that may be true, I don't think the story ends there. God knew that our sin would prevent us from being the just kings and queens He originally envisioned in our blessing. As our all-knowing, all-powerful God, He knew that various technological advances combined with unchecked greed would have the power to desolate His creation, so four curses were given out that day. He said, "cursed is the ground *because* of you."

In that sense, God didn't curse the ground, *our sin did.* Our sin and resulting behaviors are the curse for God's creation. Instead of living harmoniously with God and nature, we fight with creation and tear the ground up for our food. In other words, our free will allows us to freely destroy God's creation, even if doing so destroys ourselves.

So now you might be thinking, *"OK, so it's hopeless, right? We live in a world of sin. We were born into sin, so sinning is inevitable. And if our sin hurts creation, there's nothing we can do about that, right?"* Wrong. Just like we do not *have* to sin and can *choose* to live righteous lives, we do not *have* to lead creation-destructive lives either. "So how are we supposed to act?" The creation blessings of the Bible found in both the Old and New Testament tell us how God wants us to treat His creation. However, the noise of the world has made it hard to hear this as well.

"Dominion"

Prior to the Fall, God blessed Adam and Eve in the Garden, saying, *"Be fruitful and multiply, and fill the earth and subdue it; and have dominion over the fish of the sea and over the birds of the air and over every living thing that moves upon the earth"* (Genesis 1:28). "Subdue" and "dominion" are strong terms that seem to have confused us about our purpose in His creation.

Do you think God wants us to conquer nature and stake the flag of superiority atop the hill of His lowly creation, while we say "I'm the king of the castle and you're a dirty rascal" in a kind of nanny-nanny-boo-boo sort of way? I doubt it.

Some Christians seem to interpret God's blessing for humanity in the Garden as a free pass from God to exploit His creation for all it's worth. Think back to all that we've discussed about how deeply God knows and cares for His creation. Do you think He would go to all that trouble and then turn and say, "OK, go ahead. Wipe out entire ecosystems if it'll help your bottom line"? Again, I'm not so sure.

Some other versions of the Bible translate Genesis 1:28 in this way (emphasis added):

> **King James Version:** *And God blessed them, and God said unto them, Be fruitful, and multiply, and replenish the earth, and subdue it: and have dominion over the fish of the sea, and over the fowl of the air, and over every living thing that moveth upon the earth.*

> **New International Version:** *God blessed them and said to them, 'Be fruitful and increase in number; fill the earth and subdue it. Rule over the fish in the sea and the birds in the sky and over every living creature that moves on the ground.'*

New Life Version: *And God wanted good to come to them, saying, "Give birth to many. Grow in number. Fill the earth and rule over it. Rule over the fish of the sea, over the birds of the sky, and over every living thing that moves on the earth."*

New Living Translation: *Then God blessed them and said, "Be fruitful and multiply. Fill the earth and govern it. Reign over the fish in the sea, the birds in the sky, and all the animals that scurry along the ground."*

God gave us a big responsibility here. These translations use words associated with governments and monarchies: rule, reign, govern, dominion. Dominion is something rulers have. Kings have dominion over their kingdoms. In a sense, God is calling us to rule over the earth as kings and queens keeping things in order. But are we doing that?

To answer this question, let's look at God's instructions to Moses for how kings are *supposed* to behave:

> *When you have come into the land that the Lord your God is giving you, and have taken possession of it and settled in it, and you say, "I will set a king over me, like all the nations that are around me," you may indeed set over you a king whom the Lord your God will choose. . . . Even so, he must not acquire many horses for himself, or return the people to Egypt in order to acquire more horses . . . And he must not acquire many wives for himself, or else his heart will turn away; also silver and gold he must not acquire in great quantity for himself. When he has taken the throne of his kingdom, he shall have a copy of this law written for him in the presence of the levitical priests. It shall remain with him and he shall read in it all the days of his life, so that he may learn to fear the Lord his God, diligently observing all the words of this law and these statutes, neither exalting himself above other members of the community nor turning aside from the commandment, either to the right or to the left, so that he and his descendants may reign long over his kingdom in Israel.*
> — Deuteronomy 17: 14-20

God knew that too much gold and silver would cause a king to stray from Him. Great wealth and power cause us to feel self-sufficient and trust in all the money and all the things it can buy us, but God wants us dependent on Him instead of trusting in "stuff." To help kings keep their priorities straight, kings were also expected to read the Word of God on a daily basis to fellowship with Him and learn His character. Most importantly, God was clear that kings should not consider themselves better than their subjects.

Of course a king would *automatically* have an exalted position among the citizens and in a certain sense would be the most important individual in a kingdom. But God doesn't want the ruler to *think* of himself like that. God knew such a mindset would be dangerous for both the monarch and the subjects. When rulers look down their noses at their subjects, typically they mistreat them. If a king regards subjects as lesser, he can begin to exploit them. This is why we love stories like Robin Hood, where the just King Richard comes home to rule over the loyal subjects instead of the cruel Prince John. A king's *perspective* on his subjects makes all the difference.

Similarly, as kings and queens of creation, we are expected to rule over "*the fish of the sea, the birds of the sky, and every living creature that moves along the ground.*" We are the monarchs, and the rest of God's creatures are our subjects. Although we *automatically* have a position of authority and importance, we shouldn't *think* of ourselves that way. If we consider ourselves the *only* living things of value in creation and look down our noses at the fish of the sea, the birds of the air, and the creatures of the land, we will begin to mistreat them. Such a mindset is dangerous for both parties involved.

On the other hand, if we respect our "subjects" and view them as glorious works of our Heavenly Father, with inherent value simply because He saw fit to breathe life into them, then our behavior toward them will reflect this respect. Proverbs 12:10-11 sums up this idea nicely: "*The righteous know the needs of their animals, but the mercy of the wicked is cruel. Those who till the land will have plenty of food, but those who follow worthless pursuits have no sense.*"

Enjoyment?

Didn't God give us all things for our enjoyment, though? In Paul's first letter to the Timothy, he explains that we should set our hopes on God who *"richly provides us with all things for our enjoyment"* (1 Timothy 6:17). Indeed, there is no doubt God gave us His creation for our enjoyment. As described earlier, many Christians point to this verse as God's permission for self-indulgent, creation-destructive lifestyles.

But let me ask you this question: In the first two chapter analogies, who do you think was truly enjoying the Jones family's creation? The children in Chapter 1 playing in the back yard, making forts, and climbing trees? Or the teenage children in the second chapter "enjoying" the fruits of their parents' hard work at the party? What Allison and William did was not "enjoying" the Joneses' creation, it was exploiting it for their own selfish and short-sighted reasons. When their parents said, "Enjoy yourselves," that did not give the kids permission to disrespect their parents' possessions while the parents were away. Similarly, *"God richly provides us with everything for our enjoyment"* does not grant us permission to exploit all the natural resources of God's creation.

Still not convinced? Let's take a look at what we typically do when we truly enjoy something. Think of something you own that you really enjoy. Maybe it's your car. Let's say you worked really hard to finally save enough money to purchase it. Now you get a thrill every time you walk into the garage and turn on the ignition. Your commute has been transformed from a boring waste of time into something you look forward to each day. You *really* enjoy this car.

So what do you do with it? You keep it clean, you don't let anyone eat or smoke in it, you wash it weekly, you park at the back of the parking lot to avoid dents, you get the oil changed the minute you hit 2,000 miles. In other words, you put a lot of work into preserving and conserving it.

Enjoyment	Exploitation
When we enjoy something we: • Treasure it • Take care of it so that we can continue to enjoy it • Recognize its value • Spend time on it • Are thankful for it • Don't let others abuse it • Count the costs of using part of it • Are careful not to overdo it, because that is when enjoyment becomes a problem (like food and gluttony) • Let it bring enjoyment to others	When we exploit something we: • Use it up and then some • Come in, take what we want, get out, don't care about who's left to clean up or deal with what's left • Act like or believe it has no value • Don't care about the consequences as long as we get what we want

My point is this: when you really enjoy something, you recognize its value and you take action to preserve it the best you can so that you can *continue* to enjoy it. What if some friends were to borrow your car and brought it back to you with a ding in the door, trash in the back seat, a strange smell in the air conditioning, and the gas tank empty? Would you say they had enjoyed it? Or would "exploit" and "disrespect" be more accurate? Would you let them borrow it again?

Our *perspective* on God's creation has been skewed and twisted by our selfishness and greed. To go back to the Robin Hood analogy, instead of the conniving Prince John bent on draining his subjects of all they are worth, perhaps we should be more like King Richard, with his kind, loving, and respectful view toward his loyal subjects.

Granted, we've come a long way in the past thirty years, at least in the U.S. We're doing a much better job at conserving our environment than we did a few decades ago. But our actions on the whole indicate that we still have a long way to go.

God's Love

Now, before I go on, let me make something perfectly clear: Absolutely nothing we do could ever separate us from the love of God (Romans 8:38-39). Walter and Evelyn wouldn't stop loving Allison and William because of the party. They would certainly be angry, but that does not mean they would stop loving them. My daughter, McKenna, could burn everything I own to the ground and I would still lay down my life for her, without hesitation. However, even though my love for her wouldn't change, I would still be saddened at the loss of my home for many reasons, such as the hardships she would not have known if the hypothetical fire had not happened.

God knows that destroying aspects of His perfect creation will only bring us hardships in one way or another: increased deforestation leading to dirtier air; increased pavement leading to rising flood waters; over-fishing leading to less food. But still, despite our imperfection, despite our ongoing destruction, God loves us beyond measure, and He sent His Son to die for us—the ones He *knew* to be a curse for His creation (*"cursed is the ground because of you"*). Indeed, nothing we do could ever separate us from the love of God. And it is this perfect, unconditional love that compels me to do everything I can to please Him and try my best to live a life of which God would approve. I know many of you reading this book feel the same way. The next chapter will empower you with a biblical understanding of the relationship between our sin and creation destruction.

Lucy

In the senior parking lot of Central High School, Allison Jones gets behind the wheel of her dad's hand-me-down Ford Explorer after one of her last days of school. It's been almost two years since the party incident. Her parents had long ago forgiven her and William, the two of them had stopped hanging out with questionable characters, and William was off to college. Singing along to the radio, Allison is preoccupied with preparing for final exams. After weeks of deliberation, she has finally decided to commit to a small, out-of-state school on the west coast of Florida. While she is excited about beginning the next phase of her life, she's also very apprehensive about being that far from home, especially now that she has a new boyfriend (whom she thinks is "the one.") He is staying behind at a state school.

Will we last through college? What if I don't pass my chemistry final? What if I get really sick down at school? All these questions and more swim through her anxious teenage mind as she enters the quiet neighborhood of her childhood. The afternoon sun shines through the boughs of sweet gum trees as she rounds the turn to the back of the cul-de-sac. She sees the Thompsons out in their driveway talking and waves to her lifelong family friends.

After passing their driveway, she feels a very unfamiliar bump under her car...Immediately, she hears a sickening howling and raised voices over the noise of the radio. Horrified, Allison puts the Explorer in park and gets out to see something that would remain burned in her mind for the rest of her life: the Thompson family huddled around their beloved basset hound, Lucy, still crying out in anguish after being run over by a 2,000-pound automobile. The family initially considers rushing Lucy to the vet, but they quickly see it would be hopeless, so they sit quietly with her in the street, stroking her head as she struggles to breathe, sobbing with grief, and praying that God would take her quickly to end her suffering.

Still standing by her driver's side door with both hands gripping the sides of her face, Allison weeps as she takes all this in. When Lucy passes, Mrs. Thompson stands up and approaches her.

"Susan, I am so sorry..."

CHAPTER THREE

Changed by Love

"The freedom of the glory of the children of God"

I'd like to ask you to reflect on the sad story you just read. What did you feel as you read it? If you were Mrs. Thompson, what would you say to Allison? Of all the analogies in this book, this is the only one that has a basis in my personal experience. Later in this chapter, I will reveal what happened at the end of this tragic event. Before I do, though, I'd like you to consider something else.

So far, we've established that God takes personal ownership of His creation and that our perspectives on creation are distorted by our illusion of fulfillment. But when our behaviors cause creation destruction, what might God think? This chapter will discuss how our faulty perspectives enslave creation, and how God hears His creatures' cries for help. It's time for us to change our tune.

Bondage to Decay

"What?" you might be saying, *"Creatures' cries for help? His children have enough problems with wars, famine, poverty, and everything else. Surely God wouldn't care about silly birds and bees."* God knows our every thought, He hears our every prayer, and in His hands He holds every tear we have ever shed (Psalm 56:8). However, as discussed in Chapter 1, this does not mean that God will neglect His other creatures. As Psalm 19 describes, all of God's creation communicates with Him in voices we

cannot hear, and creation's cries about us are less than stellar.

In his letter to the Romans, Paul describes creation's longing:

> *For the creation waits with eager longing for the revealing of the children of God; for the creation was subjected to futility, not of its own will but by the will of the one who subjected it, in hope that the creation itself will be set free from its bondage to decay and will obtain the freedom of the glory of the children of God. We know that the whole creation has been groaning in labor pains until now; and not only the creation, but we ourselves, who have the first fruits of the Spirit, groan inwardly while we wait for adoption, the redemption of our bodies.* — Romans 8:19-23

In these few verses Paul packs an amazingly rich level of spiritual significance:

Creation is eagerly awaiting Christ's return and the revelation of the children of God.

Current humans (Adam's descendants) are wasting creation (subjecting it to futility).

Humans have enslaved creation with their selfish desires and creation is suffering as a result (creation's bondage to decay).

Creation's slavery is temporary and its original status that it enjoyed in the Garden will be restored at Jesus' second coming.

The children of God who are revealed after Jesus' return will treat creation as it was intended to be treated.

What's more, Paul does something unique in this passage: he personifies all of the earthly creation—all the trees, plants, water, air, soil, animals, etc.—treating each aspect as if it were a person. And Paul sees creation not as any regular person, but a person in slavery. Why else would he use such strong language as "bondage to decay?" Some translations of the Bible use the phrase "slavery of corruption," which evokes even more powerful and disturbing images. And just as in other instances of slavery, greed is the fuel and selfishness the oil that propels the engine of injustice.

But how have we enslaved creation? As discussed, our skewed perspective of God's creation has caused us to excuse away our destruction. And since all materials for the things we pursue come from the earth, this greed forces creation to give, give, give, give without any end in sight.

This lack of care for creation is evident in many of the apocalyptic verses as well. Keep in mind that "the earth" here is taken as metaphor for its human inhabitants:

- *The earth dries up and withers, the world languishes and withers; the heavens languish together with the earth. The earth lies polluted under its inhabitants; for they have transgressed laws, violated the statutes, broken the everlasting covenant. Therefore a curse devours the earth, and its inhabitants suffer for their guilt.* — Isaiah 24:4-5

- *Because you have plundered many nations, all that survive of the peoples shall plunder you—because of human bloodshed, and violence to the earth, to cities and all who live in them … The very stones will cry out from the wall, and the plaster will respond from the woodwork … For the violence done to Lebanon will overwhelm you; the destruction of the animals will terrify you—because of human bloodshed and violence to the earth, to cities and all who live in them.* — Habakkuk 2:8-17

- *So I considered my world, and saw that it was lost. I saw that my earth was in peril because of the devices of those who had come into it. And I saw and spared some with great difficulty and saved for myself one grape out of a cluster, and one plant out of a great forest.* — 2 Esdras 9:18-20

- *But the earth will be desolate because of its inhabitants, for the fruit of their doings.* — Micah 7:13

- *The nations raged, but your wrath has come, and the time for judging the dead, for rewarding your servants, the prophets and saints and all who fear your name, both small and great, and for destroying those who destroy the earth.* — Revelation 11:17-18

Now, many commentators of these verses believe the writers were speaking of moral pollution as opposed to physical pollution of natural resources. I tend to side with those who view these passages more literally. It is undeniable that we broke the covenant in the Garden. We sinned. Thus we brought a curse upon the earth, and the earth is in bondage because of it. On the other hand, everything created by God is good. Even the destructive forces of volcanoes, wildfires, and tornadoes are part of His grand plan and do good for various ecological systems. Everything touched by God or created by God is originally glorious. In this sense, God's creation is a visible manifestation of His glory, and pollution is a visible manifestation of our sin. Fortunately, though, creation's suffering will come to an end.

New Heaven and Earth

At this point, you may be wondering, "I thought we were going to get a new heaven and a new earth. What does it matter if this one is polluted? The next earth will be perfect again." On the one hand, that statement makes sense: We will receive a new heaven and earth. The book of Revelation describes what this glorious day will be like:

> Then I saw a new heaven and a new earth; for the first heaven and the first earth had passed away, and the sea was no more. And I saw the holy city, the new Jerusalem, coming down out of heaven and the first earth had passed away, and the sea was no more ... And the one who was seated on the throne said, 'See, I am making all things new ...'
> — Revelation 21:1, 5.

The prophet Isaiah foretold similar destruction and rebirth hundreds of years prior to John's Revelation:

> Now the Lord is about to lay waste the earth and make it desolate, and he will twist its surface and scatter its inhabitants. And it shall be, as with the people, so with the priest; as with the slave, so with his master; as with the maid, so with her mistress; as with the buyer, so with the seller; as with the lender, so with the borrower; as with the creditor, so with the debtor. The earth shall

be utterly laid waste and utterly despoiled; for the Lord has spoken this word.
— Isaiah 24:1-3

For I am about to create new heaven and a new earth; the former things shall not be remembered or come to mind. But be glad and rejoice forever in what I am creating; for I am about to create Jerusalem as a joy, and its people as a delight. — Isaiah 65:17-18

Yes, destruction is inevitable. God will wipe the slate clean. All of creation and the children of God will have a new heaven and a new earth when Jesus comes back.

But that's not the end of the story. As with the verses about dominion and enjoyment discussed in Chapter 2, many Christians are using these passages as excuses to live creation-sloppy lives. "Who cares if we mess up this creation? We're about to get a new one anyway." There are three major flaws with this argument.

First, as I discussed in Chapter 1, it isn't our creation. It's God's. Revisit the critical verses in the introduction for a refresher on this point if needed. The second major flaw is one of ingratitude. The "we'll get a new one anyway" mentality reminds me of situations such as these:

1. A teenager is given a smartphone and disrespects that privilege by carelessly losing it, and then comes to you as the parent and says, "Oh well, you're just going to give me another one anyway, right?" How might you feel about that?

2. A dear friend of yours is a smoker and is experiencing health problems related to smoking. The doctor tells her that she needs to quit. Later, she says to you, "Well, we're all going to die sometime. Might as well enjoy it while it lasts!" What would you say to her? Not only would she probably live longer as a non-smoker, but her quality of life would be better. What could God use her to do in that time for the Kingdom?

If those didn't hit home with you, perhaps this one will. Sometimes new Christians mistakenly think, *If Jesus is going to forgive me for my sins,*

71

then I'm just going to go ahead and live however I want. We know that is not the way to go. We cannot "take hold of the life that really is life" (1 Timothy 6:19) and live lives full of the fruit of the Spirit for the benefit of God's Kingdom if we go on sinning. This false mentality leads to diminished lives, far below the best that God has for us. Really, if you get down to it, we're only hurting ourselves. I believe the same is true for the false mentality we have about God's creation.

The third major flaw to the "we'll get a new one anyway" mentality is this: According to the Bible, we are *already* part of the new creation. Consider the following verse from the Apostle Paul: "*So if anyone is in Christ, there is a new creation: everything old has passed away; see everything has become new!*" (2 Corinthians 5:17)

According to Paul, when we accept Jesus in our hearts, we become a part of God's new creation immediately—the creation predestined for us; the one that is intended to put everything right as it was back in the Garden; the one of universal restoration; the one that all creation waits for in eager longing; the one where creation's suffering will end; the one where we will be children of God. We will retake our rightful position, not as cruel overseers of slaves, but as fair and just managers of respected individuals. Paul said that as soon as we accept Christ, we already *are* a part of this new creation.

How will we be expected to behave in this new heaven and new earth, when the children of God are revealed and the universe is restored (Acts 3:21)? The prophet Isaiah describes the new creation in this way:

> *The wolf shall live with the lamb, the leopard shall lie down with the kid, the calf and the lion and the fatling together, and a little child shall lead them. The cow and the bear shall graze, their young shall lie down together; and the lion shall eat straw like the ox. The nursing child shall play over the hole of the asp, and the weaned child shall put its hand on the adder's den. They will not hurt or destroy on all my holy mountain; for the earth will be full of the knowledge of the Lord as the waters cover the sea.*
> — Isaiah 11:6-9

What a picture of perfect peace: No one—not animals or people—will cause *any* destruction of any kind. Upon accepting Jesus and as a part of this new creation, we should "*strive to be found without spot or blemish*" (2 Peter 3:13-14), to follow Jesus, to break the bonds of our sin. To put it simply, if we are of the new creation, if we are truly the children of God, then we should protect God's creation instead of adding to its suffering.

To illustrate this point, let's revisit the wild party in Chapter 2. Imagine what your reaction would be as Mr. or Mrs. Jones if you walked in on that scene to see the broken windows, lost cat, destroyed furniture, and stained carpet. Now imagine that when you ask for an explanation, Allison and William turn to you and say, "Well, you're just going to buy us new ones anyway, right?" I don't know about you, but I would probably say something like, "Allison and William Jones, *get to your room*! Everyone else, GET OUT!!" The damage, disrespect, and disruption going on would make me want to prohibit my children from ever seeing those other teenagers again—not only because of how I value our home (our creation), but also because I know that being around those other teenagers and doing those things would be harmful to my children as well.

My point is this: William and Allison *should have known better*. As the children in that household, they should have known how their parents felt about that home, those plants, that flower bed, those pets, and so on. They certainly should have known that their parents would *not* have approved of a big party like that. But they were blinded by the illusion of fulfillment and their own selfish desires.

Still, it's hard to get past the "we'll get a new one anyway" mentality. To be honest, I've struggled with this concept myself. There are *so many* environmental problems that will require *so much* work to fix. Why put forth the effort to change our ways and lead more sustainable lives when God is just going to give us a new earth anyway?

In fact, I struggled with a similar concept even while writing this book. Why spend every morning before work writing and editing this book, taking time away from my family, if we already know that the slate will be wiped clean? But then I think of all those critical verses and especially Psalm 24:1-2. It's not my creation. It's God's. I honor God by respecting His work. The apocalypse and the following glory are imminent. But that does not mean we *have* to contribute to the problems at hand. Perhaps it's time for us to answer the numerous calls throughout the Bible, live like children of God, and sing a new song.

New Song

Over and over again, throughout Bible God calls His children to "sing a new song." These verses puzzled me in the past. One day, I asked God, "Why a *new* song? What's wrong with the old ones?" and He led me to a number of different verses throughout the Old and New Testaments.

- *Sing to the Lord a new song.* — Psalm 96

- *God put a new song in my mouth. A song of praise to our God.* — Psalm 40:3

- *Oh sing to the Lord a new song, sing to the Lord all the earth... let the heavens be glad and let the earth rejoice, let the sea roar and all that fills it, let the field exult and everything in it. Then shall all the trees of the forest sing for joy before the Lord for he is coming, for he is coming to judge the earth.* — Psalm 96: 1-3 and 11-13

- *Oh sing to the Lord a new song, for he has done marvelous things.* — Psalm 98

- *Archangels, angels, and all of creation sings the "new song" right before the seven seals are broken and judgment is handed down and God makes all things right.* — Revelation 5:9

- *Sing to the Lord a new song, his praise from the end of the earth! Let the sea roar and all that fills it, the coastlands and their inhabitants. Let the*

desert and its towns lift up their voice, the villages that Kedar inhabits; let the inhabitants of Sela sing for joy, let them shout from the tops of the mountains. Let them give glory to the Lord, and declare his praise in the coastlands. The Lord goes forth like a soldier, like a warrior he stirs up his fury; he cries out, he shouts aloud, he shows himself mighty against his foes.
— Isaiah 42:10-15

These verses have one thing in common: the authors sang a new song when God delivered them. When we go through some tremendous trial or challenge, and God sees us through to the other side, we are no longer the same. We grow stronger in faith and character, and our response to God changes. It's part of becoming a "new creation."

As soon as we choose to accept Jesus as our Savior, not only do our songs become new to God because we have been delivered, our attitude toward all of life seems new as well. The ability to sing a new song and trust God to deliver us and change our way of life is a tremendous blessing. By our free will, we can choose to accept God and sing this new song at any point.

Creation doesn't have that luxury. Like Ruban Quercus, the imaginary oak tree who wrote the letter in the beginning of this book, creation must "wait in eager longing" for the children of God to be revealed. At that point, on the last day, creation will join with us as we sing our new song of praise and thanksgiving:

For you shall go out in joy, and be led back in peace; the mountains and the hills before you shall burst into song, and all the trees of the field shall clap their hands. Instead of the thorn shall come up the cypress; instead of the brier shall come up the myrtle; and it shall be to the Lord for a memorial, for an everlasting sign that shall not be cut off. — Isaiah 55:12

I believe God wants all His children to change our tune, sing a new song, and respect His creation for the masterful work of art that it is, in all our daily choices and actions.

Changed by Love

As we draw near to the conclusion to the first part of this book, I'd like to repeat a point from the introduction: I'm not suggesting that we all become Amish, live in trees, or go back to a hunter/gatherer subsistence style of living. I think God is trying to show where we are missing the mark in terms of our *perspective* or *attitude* toward His creation. I know from the depths of my soul that He wants us to respect His creation. But how you change your actions as a result of gaining that respect is between you and God. Still, I realize that changing perspective is difficult, to say the least. With that in mind, I'd like to take you back to Allison Jones.

At the beginning of this chapter, you read a sad story about Allison accidentally running over the Thompson family's beloved basset hound. As mentioned earlier, of all the parables in this book, this is the only one that is based on a story from my life—and one of my biggest regrets.

When I was a senior in high school, I ran over Lucy on my way home from school one day. On that afternoon, my neighbors were standing in their driveway talking and watching Lucy (who was almost blind and mostly deaf from old age) sniff around in the yard. As I rounded the turn at their house, I waved to the family in the driveway, not realizing that the sun on my windshield and the mottled shadows through the trees colored the road to camouflage sweet Lucy from sight. Immediately, I jumped out of the car to witness the family huddled around poor Lucy as she struggled to breathe her last and howled in pain.

Even though this dog was not one of their children (thank God!!) and even though the Thompsons were not the ones physically suffering, it was obvious that the family shared in Lucy's pain. They had loved her for more than 13 years. They had fed her every day, taken her to the vet when she was sick, played with her for countless hours, and laughed as they watched her short legs bounding through the snow after a rare Georgia snowstorm. To this day, Lucy's doghouse still stands in their yard with her name above the door, memorializing their lost pet.

Just like my neighbors who loved Lucy so much, I believe God reveals His heart to us for His creatures in our own love and devotion to our pets. When His creatures suffer, God hears their cry and wants it to stop. My childhood neighbors wanted to take Lucy's pain away, and if they could have had her back and restored her to the healthy happy dog they knew in her youth, I'm sure they would have.

However, the story doesn't end there. There is one part of the introductory metaphor that didn't happen. The "Thompson" family *did* rush to Lucy's side—all but one of them, that is. As I stood there with my hands over my face, weeping, shaking and trying to say something that would make things better, Mrs. Thompson walked right past Lucy. She came up to me and began *comforting me*. I would have *totally* understood if she had shouted at me, cursed my head off, or bashed in my windshield with a baseball bat. Instead, she held me in her arms and sought to comfort me, reminding me how old Lucy was, how she was blind and running into walls, and so on.

In that moment, Mrs. Thompson did more to demonstrate the love of God to me than anyone else had up to that point. Of course, she adored Lucy and didn't want her to suffer—as the Bible indicates God doesn't want His creatures to suffer. Seeing the deep remorse in my face, however, she instantly forgave me and tried to help me forgive myself. God does the same for His children. Did I remember that moment for the rest of my life? Yes. Do I think about it every time I see a basset hound or sweet Lucy's little doghouse? Yes. Did it make me a more cautious driver, especially in residential areas? Absolutely.

My point is this: Out of love for the Thompsons, I never wanted to cause them that kind of pain again, even though they forgave me. The same should go for how we treat God's creation. Yes, He will forgive His children no matter what. We could nuke the whole thing to deep space, and He would never stop loving us. But out of that knowledge of His love and out of respect for Him, we should respond to His creation with reverence and respect.

This is the heart of "How we're missing the mark" when it comes to God's creation, which has been Part I of this book. The remaining chapters will discuss how we might respond to this love and live scripture-informed, creation-respecting lifestyles, starting with our reverence for creation's Biblical value.

PART TWO

THE SCRIPTURE-INFORMED CREATION-RESPECTING LIFE

A Tale of Two Marshes...

Marsh One

"Look at it all!" John Covax says to his friend and business partner, Peter Sable, with arms stretching out over a lush, green salt marsh. The sun glints off the high tide between waving blades of tall grass dotted with periwinkle snails. It is 10 o'clock on a June morning, and the intensity of the South Georgia heat is beginning to pick up. Peter, who is sometimes less enthusiastic than John, sits on a stump fanning himself with a "Welcome to the Golden Isles" brochure. His excited friend talks with his hands with such fervor that he appears to be standing in one of those dollar-grab machines on a TV game show. Peter just tries to humor him.

John and Peter have known each other a long time. They grew up just a few counties over from here, where they still live and attend the same church every Sunday. When they reunited after college, they decided to use Peter's engineering skills and John's business prowess to go into the chemical business together. This decision has proven lucrative for them both, and their business continues to grow. Their chemical products help a tremendous number of people and do a world of good. Still, wanting to stay ahead of the curve, they are here today looking for ways to expand their business.

"About 70 feet down in this marsh lies a huge reserve of phosphates," John explains to his partner. "Phosphates are used in everything from dish detergents, to water treatment, to flame retardants, to metal polishes...I mean, no plant can grow without phosphates, so it's included in every kind of fertilizer. Think of all the good it could do and the big return we could get from all the products!"

After a pause, Peter asks his partner, "When will we find out if the state has granted us the mineral lease to begin dredging?"

A Tale of Two Marshes...

Marsh Two

Struggling for breath, a 35-year-old man hobbles into a maritime forest late one June morning, his worn leather shoes shuffling through decaying leaves and Spanish moss as he approaches an old live oak. He leans his thin shoulder against the tree as his body succumbs to a fit of painful coughing. He feels dizzy. He has little choice but to sit and rest.

As he lowers himself down, he tries to remind himself that today is a pretty good day. Despite the terminal illness that causes frequent hemorrhages, and despite the emotional burdens he carries as a veteran and former prisoner of war, he has walked here on his own, making today better than many he has seen recently.

Still, the weight of the world is on his shoulders. He and his family struggle financially. This is mainly due to the fact that his expansive interests—music, law, natural history, education, literature—caused him to bounce from job to job in his younger years and prevented him from accruing a financial safety net. Now he is too sick to hold a steady job.

His past was not without opportunities, though. He gave up

a lucrative career in his father's law office and turned down multiple offers for military advancement during the war. The worldly possessions and financial security those opportunities would have provided would have been an even greater burden than the one he experiences now.

No, he knew at a young age that his path was not of this world. God gave him eyes to see the world in a new way and a mind for putting these divine messages into songs and poems. To deny this deep-rooted passion that set his soul on fire would have been equivalent to emotional, spiritual, and possibly even literal suicide.

His "holy obligation," as he calls it, has brought him back time and again to get these messages out to the world. Inspiration seems to scream at him a hundred times a day: sitting at the doctor's office, driving down the road, or having dinner with his family. But nowhere is this creative voice clearer than out in secluded, natural settings.

The trouble is, no one seems to be listening. Before leaving the house today he had to reassure his wife that art and rejection go hand in hand, and that it was only a matter of time before one of these publishers would see the immense value of his work. Of this he has no doubt, but he secretly fears that recognition will come posthumously.

Still, despite the rejections, he remains full to the brim with life-changing ideas and he knows in his heart of hearts that he has the capacity to bring them to fruition—or he would, if only he had the funds and the health.

If only...

The fact remains that he struggles to feed and clothe his children, struggles to suppress the horrors of war in his mind, and frequently struggles to take his next breath. At times, these struggles absolutely overwhelm him.

Sitting against that live oak, he closes his eyes to try and hide from the struggles for a moment. He leans his head back against the strong old oak as if hoping his problems would soak into the tree; but he finds no relief. All that has happened roars through his mind and eclipses any feeble efforts to be quieted.

The worst part is that he knows that the goal of today's trip to the forest is within reach. The problem is that his arms are too busy swatting away the swarm of angry bees in his mind to reach for the honey. In desperation, he begins to pray. He asks God for healing from his ailments, relief from financial burdens, and reassurance that he is on the right path with his work.

"Please, God," he begs, "I know you gave me these gifts for a reason—an incredibly important reason. Why, God? Why give me such powerful revelations in my work if I'm only going to receive one rejection letter after another? What am I doing wrong? What do you want me to do?" The tears flow freely now as he cries out to God in devoted frustration, and then...

Through his tears his mind wanders back to the oak supporting him. The deep ridges of the bark, harder and rougher than a paved road, dig grooves into his back. With a trunk wider than three of him, the strong old oak feels like a mighty fortress compared to his frail body. A memory of his father at the dinner table reading the creation verses from the Good Book comes to mind. He tries to imagine God creating the majestic tree from nothing. Wiping the tears from his eyes, he looks up into the twisting branches.

Unlike their straight-branched cousins, the boughs of live oaks twist and bend like gnarled, arthritic fingers, offering winding highways for the rising Ascension Ferns and sturdy anchors for the dripping grey bundles of Spanish Moss. The noonday sun tries in vain to push its way down through the branches that reach out and intermingle with the next tree, arching over the green underbrush. The effect of the light through this cacophony of green reminds him less of a simple forest canopy and more of a stained glass window. The beauty and simplicity of that scene above him give him pause.

Wiping the remainder of the tears from his cheeks, a thought comes to him: he is not in a simple forest, but in a church. Not one built with brick and mortar, but a house of worship crafted by the Creator Himself. This is a beautiful, living, breathing, growing cathedral, and he is a part of it: living, breathing, and growing right along with it.

Most of all, he sees himself not as a man sitting against a tree, but as a humble, repentant, loving child kneeling at a pew. And like any good church, this house of worship offers him not only an escape from the world, but a challenge to come up higher, think differently, and live a more righteous life. The peace that washes over him feels as if God has handed him a beekeeper's suit, equipping him to press on toward his goal.

So grateful for this moment, he stays there all day allowing the unexpected moment of worship to soak in as he calibrates his compass within. He wants to hold on to these feelings, to make sense of this experience. Fervently he scribbles down his thoughts. In one set of scribbles, he realizes that a God of such power, such might, and such wisdom, who could create such a perfect place as this, knows all about the troubles in his life—troubles that now seems somehow less significant.

The Creator is an all-knowing, all-powerful, all-present God. He not only <u>knows</u> of these problems, but He is <u>using</u> them to make this frail and insignificant man into a mighty warrior for His kingdom. The man finds himself declaring out loud, "All things work together for good for those who love God and are called according to His purpose!"

A glint of sunlight interrupts the man's thoughts. He sets down his pen. Looking to the east he sees the "altar" of this earthen house of worship: the expansive salt marsh. With some effort, he stands and slowly walks to the edge of the forest as if drawn by an invisible string. In the late afternoon sun, the marsh shines in the sun like a beacon of hope. Remembering his natural history lessons, he thinks about the hardy creatures that live in the grasses below.

One of the harshest habitats in the world, the marshes endure daily cycles of grueling flooding with brackish water, scorching dry conditions between the tides, and the full force of this oppressive Georgia sun.

Despite this abuse, these grasses produce four times more biomass than the most efficient corn fields and serve as a nursery for the fish that feed Georgia's people. And if that weren't enough, they also protect the mainland from violent tidal surges, hurricanes, and the roaring surf. What would be torture for most creatures, God had turned into life-giving harmony.

Thinking of this paradox and looking out over the marsh, the man thinks once more of the life-giving sacrifice made by another long ago; and a wave of overwhelming gratitude floods over him. This renewed devotion to his Savior gives him courage to press on to the other side of the marsh until he steps out on the firm packed sand.

Free.

Closing his eyes once more, he hears the mighty roar of the ocean and feels of the wind blow through his soul like the songs of angels. Deeply moved, he opens his eyes and gazes out over the vastness of the Atlantic.

In every direction stands another divine paradox of pure, deep blue: seemingly simple, yet infinitely complex; phenomenally beautiful, yet surpassingly powerful and dangerous. His soul hungers for more: more of this power, more of this beauty, this simplicity within infinite complexity, more knowledge of God.

Renewed and empowered with purpose, the man returns to his home where he immortalizes his experience in a grateful ode to the "wide sea-marshes of Glynn."

CHAPTER FOUR

Creation's Biblical Value

Preserve creation for God's glory

I once watched a program about how much the Earth is worth. In this documentary, the filmmakers tallied up the value of all the trees, metals, water, fossil fuels, etc. across the entire planet. While these kinds of programs are interesting, they are also a good example of how we typically think of God's creation: short-sighted and selfishly. What's in it for us? What's the bottom line?

Very rarely do we stop and recognize the value of nature for what it can do *in* us. Certainly resources in God's creation have monetary value and there is nothing wrong with buying and selling. God understands that we have needs and He uses creation to help us meet our needs. However, an issue arises when we move past the meeting of needs.

Just as a church is worth far more than the cost of the bricks, wood, and other supplies that went into building it, God's creation as a whole is worth far more than the monetary value that can be gained from its natural resources. By cherishing and honoring God's creation, and looking past short-sighted gains, we can begin to see creation's biblical value: to protect us, communicate with us, have fellowship with us, and prepare us for His Kingdom.

In this sense, the biblical values of creation come together in four levels of increasing complexity, importance, and depth of understanding:

91

Level 1: Survival

Level 2: Realization of God

Level 3: Spiritual Development

Level 4: Glorifying God

In order to become the stewards of creation that God intended us to be—those who "till and keep" the Garden (Genesis 2:15), we need to progress beyond the lower, more superficial levels and respect God's masterpiece with the honor it deserves.

Level 1: Survival

Take a deep breath. The most obvious value of creation (from a human perspective at least), and the most basic reason God gave us this planet, is for our survival. Even right now, as you are reading this book, you are breathing in little doses of atmospheric gases in the exact combinations needed for survival: about 78 percent nitrogen and 20 percent oxygen. Adjust those percentages even a few percentage points, and we begin to struggle. Yet all around the world, God keeps the air we breathe in the right proportions for the life that lives there. The atmospheres of other planets are *nothing* like this one. We are exactly the right distance from the sun and rotate at exactly the right speed with exactly the right combinations of trees, volcanic gases, and water to keep the system working.

In Eric Metaxas' *Wall Street Journal* article "Science increasingly makes the case for God," he explains that in order to support life, a planet must have not only "the right kind of star and a planet the right distance from that star" but far, far more:

> Today there are more than 200 known parameters necessary for a planet to support life—every single one of which must be perfectly met, or the whole thing falls apart. Without a massive

planet like Jupiter nearby, whose gravity will draw away asteroids, a thousand times as many would hit Earth's surface. The odds against life in the universe are simply astonishing.

Metaxas sums up his point beautifully in this way: "the odds against the universe existing are so heart-stoppingly astronomical that the notion that it all 'just happened' defies common sense. It would be like tossing a coin and having it come up heads 10 quintillion times in a row."

We take it for granted, but in reality, every breath, every heartbeat, every second of life is a tiny miracle. Move the planet a little farther away, cause it to rotate a little slower, or change even one of the 200 required parameters for life and we might not be able to take that breath. Only God in His infinite wisdom and power could combine the forces surrounding us in the exact ratios to enable that next breath.

But He doesn't stop there. The food we eat, the water that sustains us, the shelters that protect us from the elements, all come from the hand of our indescribable Creator. Not one single moment of life would be possible without God and His unimaginable gift of creation. Even if we offered a prayer of thanksgiving every time our hearts beat throughout our entire lives, we wouldn't begin to come close to giving Him enough credit and gratitude for this incredible, life-giving gift. Recognizing creation as God's indescribable, consummate, perfect gift of love and wisdom is the first step or level of realizing creation's biblical value.

Level 2: Realization of God

To illustrate the second level of creation appreciation, consider the reverence for creation found in other indigenous populations all over the globe. From Native Americans to aboriginal tribes in Australia, the natural world is seen as sacred. For example, in Chief Seattle's response to the American government's offer to purchase their indigenous lands in the 1800s, he explained how the concept of buying and selling the land was so strange to them:

> The President in Washington sends word that he wishes to buy our land. But how can you buy or sell the sky? The land? The idea is strange to us. If we do not own the freshness of the air and the sparkle of the water, how can you buy them? Every part of the earth is sacred to my people. Every shining pine needle, every sandy shore, every mist in the dark woods, every meadow, every humming insect. All are holy in the memory and experience of my people.[2]

This kind of reverence for creation is difficult for modern-day Christians to understand. Imagine that someone came up to you and wanted to buy something of God's that you unknowingly had in your possession. You would look at that person as if he or she had two heads. Yet this divine respect for creatures can be found all over the world because God reveals Himself to the masses through nature. It is absolutely astounding how distant communities of ancient peoples ame to similar realizations about the existence of the divine simply from observing nature. Granted, these ancient communities interpreted the creation message differently than the Bible instructs (nature idolatry, pantheism, etc.). As C. S. Lewis observed, these ancient religions were "echoes or anticipations" of the full Truth in Jesus Christ.[3] When you hear an echo, it's sometimes difficult to decipher its exact message. If it hadn't been for God hard-wiring us for Him through creation, if He hadn't laid this key foundation in the hearts and minds of these peoples, much of the missionary work over the past two millennia may not have been possible.

This is exactly what Paul was talking about in his letter to the Romans: *Ever since the creation of the world, His eternal power and divine nature, invisible though they are, have been understood and seen through the things He has made* (Romans 1:20). King David proclaimed something similar in his 19th Psalm: *The heavens are telling the glory of God; and the firmament proclaims his handiwork . . . There is no speech, nor are there words; their voice is not heard; yet*

---

2 Chief Seattle, *"Letter to the American Government,"* in http://www.csun.edu/~vcpsy00h/seattle.htm
3 Allister McGrath, *C. S. Lewis: A Life* (Alive Communications, Inc., 2013), 150-151.

their voice goes out through all the earth, and their words to the end of the world. (v. 1-4)

As Christians we are blessed to have the whole story. However, many of us now have ears deaf to God's voice resounding off His creation. Recognizing creation as a loudspeaker for God's existence and treating it with the reverence such a medium deserves is the second level of realizing creation's biblical value.

Level 3: Spiritual Development

Creation can become even more meaningful for those who have an awareness of God and respect Him for His works. God uses nature as a tool for our spiritual development through communication and character development.

Communication: First, communication with God can be easier in a natural setting. In crowded, manmade settings where hustle and bustle are at their peak, it gets more and more difficult to hear that still, small voice. Have you ever noticed how we like to take vacations to places where creation has a central focus? It's easier to relax, recharge, and refocus near the ocean, by a lake house, or in a secluded mountain cabin. We say, "It's so peaceful here," and enjoy the tranquility and serenity. When we "get away from it all," we feel refreshed afterward. I believe this is an example of God using creation to speak to us, reminding us what is most important. When we are surrounded by things God made, the noise starts fading away.

Character: Creation helps us understand God's character. The beauty, power, and complexity of nature mirrors the beauty, power, and complexity of God. Spending time in nature and learning about its intricacies can help us understand God better, which develops our character. Paradoxically, the serenity and tranquility of nature remind us to "be still," yet nature's seemingly violent aspects also bring us to a better awareness of Him. Natural phenomena such as earthquakes, hurricanes, and volcanoes give us tiny glimpses of His all-encompassing and surpassing power and might. Such natural phenomena humble us and force us to come to terms with our limited capacity. What's more, in the amazing complexity that makes up the balance of forces in every ecosystem God reveals glimpses of His divine wisdom.

When we seek out nature for some quiet time and communication with God and learn of God's power and complexity by "lifting our eyes unto the hills," we have reached the third level of realizing creation's biblical value. As the wise King Solomon said,

> *And if people were amazed at their power and working, let them perceive from them how much more powerful is the one who formed them. For from the greatness and beauty of created things comes a corresponding perception of their creator.* — Wisdom of Solomon 13:4-5

Level 4: Creation Glorifies God

Once you see creation as a visible manifestation of God's glory and spend time in nature growing in communication with Him, you come to the final and most important level of creation appreciation: experiencing the glory of God. But some of you may be wondering, what exactly is glory? I know there are many definitions, and there are certainly many facets of God's glory; but I'd like to share a memory from my prayer life to help explain one aspect in particular.

I asked God once to let me understand me what "glory" meant to Him and what was so great about it. Instantly, interactions I had had with nature came to mind: The night hike on Sapelo Island Beach when I came across a mother sea turtle laying her eggs; walking in Muir Woods amidst a cathedral of massive trees that breathed the same air as Jesus when they were saplings 2,000 years ago; the time in Maui when I got so sunburned because I refused to move from one spot on the boat for fear of missing a breeching humpback whale; or the time at summer camp when a group of 10 twelve-year-old campers broke down in unexplainable weeping when walking into an open-air chapel overlooking an ancient mountain range. Every one of those instances filled me with awe and wonder for my Creator—my Master—at the sight of His masterpieces.

What I think God was revealing to me in those moments is this: in this sense, creation can be seen as a visible manifestation of God's power, beauty, complexity, wisdom—His visible glory. Every rock, every tree, every bird, every coral, every grain of sand, every ant is a little loudspeaker of the glory of God simply because God made it. With our free will and the level of "noise" around us, God's glory is not always *obvious* to us, so having creation act as a visible reminder of glory is helpful.

Level 4: Value Examples

So what does Level 4 creation appreciation look like? Are there examples in the Bible? Yes. A few Bible figures seem to stand out as leaders in valuing creation as God's masterpiece.

For example, Vineyard Boise Pastor Tri Robinson called Noah the 'consummate conservationist' because of his work to rescue all animal life on the planet.[4] Moses dutifully followed God's instructions about crop rotation (Leviticus 25:1-7) to prevent the soil from becoming decimated of its nutrients. King David's love and respect for creation is crystal clear in the Psalms.

But the one old testament example that stands out in my mind is that of King Solomon. When God promised to give Solomon anything he asked for, he made a specific request for *"an understanding mind to govern your people, able to discern between good and evil"* (1 Kings 3:9). God granted Solomon's request and included wisdom for the natural world:

> *God gave Solomon very great wisdom, discernment and breadth of understanding as vast as the sand on the seashore, so that Solomon's wisdom surpassed the wisdom of all the people of the East, and all the wisdom of*

---

4 Tri Robinson, *Saving God's Green Earth: Rediscovering the Church's Responsibility to Environmental Stewardship,* Norcross, GA: Ampelon Publishing, 2006.

Egypt ... He would speak of trees, from the cedar that is in the Lebanon to the hyssop that grows in the wall; he would speak of animals, and birds, and reptiles, and fish. People came from all the nations to hear the wisdom of Solomon; they came from all the kings of the earth who had heard of his wisdom. — 1 Kings 4: 29-34

Such understanding would be useful when it came to keeping workers safe from harm while they built the grand temple of God. For example, borrowing from current knowledge of major construction concerns, he could have used that creation wisdom to strategically cut or purchase the cedar and cypress (1 Kings 5:6) without causing landslides, to quarry stone for the walls and foundation (1 Kings 5:17), and to mine the gold for the inner room (1 Kings 6:21) without poisoning the water supply.

However, of all the Level 4 creation respecting examples in the Bible, Jesus provides the most powerful example. On many occasions throughout the Gospel, Jesus sought out natural settings in which to pray by himself. I'm sure this choice was partly due to the fact that he needed relief from human distraction, but an empty room and a closed door could have provided the same.

I believe Jesus knew that creation is an effective place to really "be still"—surrounded by nothing but God's work. Interestingly, the times he sought nature solitude were before major miracles or big decisions: before feeding the 5,000 (Matthew 14:13); before walking on water (Matthew 14:23); before the transfiguration (Matthew 17:1); before choosing his disciples (Luke 5:16, 6:12); and in the Garden at Gethsemane.

Jesus "lived lightly upon the earth," also, as Art and Jocele Meyer describe in their book *Earthkeepers*[5]. In his wisdom and humility, Jesus only took what he needed to survive. Instead of expecting more stuff and more money to give him happiness and taking more from creation than was necessary, he said, "*Life does not consist of the abundance*

---

5 Art and Jocele Meyer, *Earthkeepers: Environmental Perspectives on Hunger, Poverty, and Injustice.* Pennsylvania, Herald Press, 1991.

of possessions." (Luke 12:15) Although we have no way of knowing exactly what Jesus was doing in all those instances of creation-solitude, I imagine that he took pleasure in the creatures around him. I bet he stopped to admire passing butterflies, smelled the fragrant flowers, relished the cool spring waters over his tired feet, and admired His Father's noble trees. I wonder if He could hear "the rocks crying out" to him or the fields singing for joy in those instances. What glory he must have experienced!

Progressing in Creation Appreciation

So let's take a step back. Now that we've discussed the four levels and looked at biblical examples, ask yourself where you fall on the spectrum. As with all aspects of spiritual development, when we approach Level 4 creation appreciation, God has a way of changing our perspectives on the way the world works. We begin to see how various aspects of nature are little containers reflecting God's glory. This new perspective causes us to appreciate creation in a new way because to know nature is to love creation. Those wildflowers you never noticed before are now amazingly beautiful. Those birds in your backyard feed your soul with creator-inspired music.

As individuals, little by little you may become aware of all the ways that your actions and the actions of those around you are harming God's masterpieces. Gradually, out of love and respect for God, creation-harmful actions may not sit well with you anymore. You may start to change behaviors that are not in line with your new perspectives. Perhaps throwing that soda can out of the car window isn't as easy any more. Perhaps you notice just how many bags of trash you go through in a week. Or perhaps you become increasingly frustrated with creation destruction around you.

Calvin DeWitt illustrates this beautifully in his acclaimed book *Earthwise: A Guide To Hopeful Creation Care*[6]:

6Calvin DeWitt, *Earthwise: A Guide To Hopeful Creation Care*. Faith Alive Christian Resources, 2011.

We can think of any of the world's great libraries as a great treasure house of recorded learning and knowledge. Imagine, though, that we come upon a library without understanding or caring about reading its texts. Imagine that we might not even know that the printed characters in its books make up words and sentences. Suppose also that—not recognizing these as stores of knowledge—we view these books as fuel, nicely packaged and arranged in neat stacks for us to use in our wood-burning stoves! (p.86-87)

Once we recognize the tremendous value of God's masterpieces, wasting them begins to seem outrageous.

Perhaps you are saying to yourself, *"I'm a Christian, but this whole 'Level 4' thing seems a bit extreme. I don't know if I can do that."* If that sentiment describes you, I ask only one thing of you: follow Jesus' example and spend time with God in nature.

As Christians, we are supposed to follow Jesus and live like Him in all aspects. Yes, "love one another" is the most important commandment, and going to church is critical for our spiritual development. But if we are trying to truly follow Jesus, perhaps we should follow his nature-solitude example as well.

How would the world be different if all Christians modeled Jesus' prayer life, in addition to his acts of love for others, and experienced the wilderness alone? How many of God's glory-giving masterpieces could we preserve? How many more people would be drawn to Him in this industrial world as a result of creation's inherent grandeur?

The Level 4 Difference

Human actions can glorify God as well. Helping a friend in need, renouncing harmful habits and going to church, working to help the hurting and the needy: all of these acts point people in the direction of God and give Him the credit He deserves. Still there's something extra special, extra awe-inspiring, extra glorious about His wondrous creation, the beauty and grandeur which draw people to Him automatically (Level 2).

But the Level 4 difference comes in when that instinctual inclination toward Him is combined with the biblical awareness of His loving works and dedication for us. That's when our souls can't help but sing to God and give Him glory, like the old hymn sums up perfectly:

> *O Lord my God, When I in awesome wonder consider all the worlds thy hand has made, I see the stars, I hear the rolling thunder, Thy power throughout the universe displayed. Then sings my soul, my savior God to thee, How great thou art. How great thou art.* — Pastor Carl Boberg[7]

When our soul "sings" like the hymn says, we begin to understand that giving God glory is more than just an act or something we *do*, it's also something we *feel* and something we *know*. It's a love song from our souls to the creator of the universe. It's the most natural thing in the world. It's our true home. Creation helps us tap into that song of love.

On a side note, we do not glorify God because God is some egotistical being who just wants to hear how great He is. Glorifying God is for *our* benefit—it puts all the other silly things we worry about into perspective when we acknowledge him and receive His love.

God doesn't *need* anything from us. Nevertheless, He *wants* fellowship with us. When we cease to resist Him and grant Him that request, we can receive His peace and be joyful. In other words, when we glorify God, when we really sing our soul song to Him, we experience a little piece of heaven.

This is the reason why we feel drawn to landscapes like the Grand Canyon or a beautiful mountain overlook. We all have an inherent hunger for God, and we sense the Master through His masterpieces.

---

7 "How Great Thou Art: The history of the hymn," accessed March 15, 2016, http:// www.allaboutgod.com/how-great-thou-art.htm

Keep It Good

To know nature is to love God's creation. To love God's creation is to preserve it. To preserve creation is to preserve a piece of God's visible glory on Earth. To preserve creation is to honor God.

***

Earlier, I described two perspectives on a salt marsh. In the first, two men hoped to receive a mineral lease that would allow them to strip-mine the marsh for phosphates. In the second, a sick man found comfort and divine revelation just from sitting on the edge of the marsh and contemplating the greatness of God.

Both of these scenarios are based on true stories about the same marsh in Glynn County, Georgia, but they took place about 100 years apart. In 1968, the Kerr-McGee Corporation wanted to strip-mine the marshes of Georgia's Golden Isles for an estimated 800 million tons of phosphate. At the time, Georgia's governor asked the U.S. Geological Survey to do an investigation on the marshes and ultimately Georgia's legislature decided to turn them down.

The second marsh story was based on Georgia's most famous poet, Sidney Lanier. Lanier found his way to the Glynn County coast and wrote *"The Marshes of Glynn"* in 1878 as he was dying of tuberculosis and at his financial wit's end. Arguably Lanier's best work, this poem touched the lives of millions and brought many of its readers closer to the One that matters most. What powerful images it evokes when reading it: survival, connection, communication, and fellowship. As Susan Copeland explains:

> Lanier found his purest voice in the religious vision of 'The Marshes of Glynn,' which was inspired by a visit to Brunswick ... He feels himself growing and connecting with the sinews of the marsh itself ... Then as the vision expands seaward, he recognizes in an epiphany moment that the marshes and sea, in their vastness, are an expression of the 'greatness of God'.[8]

---

8 "Sidney Lanier (1842-1881)," Susan Copeland 2002, retrieved from: georgiaencyclopedia.org/articles/arts-culture/sidney-lanier-1842-1881

I am so thankful the Georgia legislature voted to turn down the mining company. What a different place Georgia's "Golden Isles" would be! I cannot help but wonder if Lanier's poem was also ringing in the ears of those legislators, many of whom may have memorized parts of it as schoolchildren. Thank God, because of that legislative decision, new generations can grow in creation appreciation through the salt marshes as Lanier did so long ago.

***

Creation glorifies God. We sense this when we stand before mighty mountains or a roaring ocean. Creation is God's magnet for souls. Creation knows its purpose. We're the ones who are confused, and we get more and more confused as we get further and further immersed in the noise of this world. Everyone suffers from the loss of God's handiwork, His masterpieces. However, as I will discuss in the next chapter, the poor are the ones who feel the effects of creation destruction first and hardest. Preserving God's creation is one of the most effective ways to care for the least

And [Now] Who is My Neighbor?

There was once a remote community in a developing country. The villagers sustained themselves by farming their fertile lands and fishing in the nearby river. Foreign agricultural corporations heard of the fertile soil and moved into the region. In a matter of years, the corporations polluted the rivers with factory waste and destroyed the soil by overworking the fields and overusing chemical pesticides and fertilizers. Robbed of their ability to sustain themselves, the villagers were now on the brink of starvation.

A foreign church heard of their struggles and sent the whole community meals for a week. While the villagers appreciated the food, the town quickly returned to desperation. So likewise, a humanitarian group came with food and a medical team, but they left after a few weeks. Distended bellies, exposed ribs, and sunken eyes quickly returned after the group's departure as starvation loomed once more.

Finally, a group of humanitarian scientists came to the town with food, water, medicine, and a host of testing kits. In addition to meeting the town's immediate needs, they ran a series of tests on the community's natural resources. They started with the soil, where they found toxic levels of fertilizers and pesticides, so they dug up the top soil and put down natural compost with hearty grasses intended to rejuvenate nutrients. To prevent future destruction, they taught the farmers about crop rotation and the dangers of overusing chemical farming agents. Next, they tested the village's river water and found high levels of bacteria from animal waste. They went to all the farms in the area and taught the farmers about the importance of livestock buffer zones. They traveled upstream to make sure other farming towns did the same. After a while, they re-stocked the river and held seminars about sustainable fishing practices in the community. Gradually, the villagers of the remote community began to regain their health and lives.

Now, which of these, do you think, was a neighbor to that community?

CHAPTER FIVE

"Give a Man a Fish"

Serving the least through creation care

We've all heard the old adage: *"Give a man a fish, feed him for the day. Teach a man to fish, feed him for life."* Without a doubt, those are words of wisdom to be cherished.

But in today's world, these wise words are only true if there are fish in the river. I think we could add to this adage: *"Give a man clean water and sustainable fishing practices, feed his whole village for generations."* What's more, the opposite is also true: *"Steal a man's fish, he'll go hungry for a day. Steal a man's river, he'll go hungry for a lifetime."*

In our mission work, we're good at "giving the man a fish," and we even do a pretty good job of "teaching the man to fish." However, in our daily life choices, many of us are "stealing the man's river" without even realizing it. We are supposed to love the least and take care of those who are poor and hungry.

But what if protecting the poor's natural surroundings could *prevent* many of those needs in the first place? This chapter will examine the modern definition of "neighbor" and how restoring and protecting God's creation is one of the best ways to serve the least.

New "Neighbor"

If you have been a Christian for a while, you probably recognized the inspiration behind this chapter's metaphor: Jesus' parable of the Good Samaritan (Luke 10:25-37). This passage has inspired countless acts of love and selflessness over thousands of years and brought millions of people to Christ for the glory of God. It defines one of our major assignments as the body of Christ in the world, and we have responded to this call with gusto. We've built hospitals, orphanages, homeless shelters, and countless other institutions to assist the sick and needy. We've sent mission teams all over the globe to continue God's work, meet people's needs, and share the gospel of Jesus Christ. I have no doubt that God is pleased with all of these righteous and noble efforts. What's more, if the introductory interpretation of this key passage was a true story, I have no doubt that Jesus would be happy with the efforts of the first two groups in the story above.

However, I can't help but wonder: if Jesus told us the parable of the Good Samaritan today, would it be *exactly* like his original? In Jesus' time, the average person typically traveled no farther than about 30 miles from his or her home. Everything people needed came from resources found in and around their community. In most cases, the impact of a person's life did not stretch very far, so a "neighbor" was a very concrete and tangible relationship.

Today things are much more complicated and the reach of one person goes much, much farther. People travel far and wide for business, recreation, and necessity with modern transportation. When you walk into a typical supermarket, you might find a tiny section of locally sourced produce, but the vast majority of the items are shipped in, sometimes from halfway across the planet. Just look at shellfish: almost all of the shrimp Americans consume come from aquaculture farms in Asia.

Every dollar we spend has an impact somewhere, so every time we purchase an imported item, that purchase has an impact on its place of origin in one way or another. We may not realize it, but the reach of one life today is exponentially farther than it was in Jesus' time. Being a "neighbor" has a very different meaning today than it did for Jesus' audience in Luke 10.

Now, the 21st century interpretation of the Good Samaritan on the previous pages is not a perfect analogy since the Priest and the Levite in Jesus' parable did nothing, and the first two groups in the story tried to help the village, at least. Either way, (and this is key here) the Samaritan in Jesus' story didn't just throw band-aids at the man and move on to the next guy in the ditch. He stuck with the victim until the problem was fixed so he could get back on his feet and go about his life *without* the Samaritan. Jesus doesn't say where the Samaritan went the next day, but I like to think that he went to the powers-that-be to try and improve security on the road to Jericho and really tackle the problem at its source.

It seems that many Christian and humanitarian groups (though definitely not all) are choosing more of a Band-Aid option when it comes to humanitarian missions. Their impact may be far-reaching geographically, but shallow in addressing the root of the problem. Since our "neighbors" have changed since Jesus' time, so must our mission work and daily life choices change as well. But before we get to that, let's examine the reasons why the changes are needed in the first place.

Why the Least Need a Healthy Creation
(and everyone else does too)

God gave us this planet to help us live and survive. Every tiny piece of creation—every plant, every insect, every animal—works together like a great machine designed to make air, food, clothing, and everything else we need. Just like Mr. and Mrs. Jones in Chapter 1 provided William and Allison a safe and nurturing home, God uses His creation to support and care for all of His children. In His infinite wisdom, God built in all the utility services we need.

To illustrate this point, consider the following from renowned Harvard ecologist E. O. Wilson. In his book *The Future of Life,* Wilson describes water filtration, food production, erosion control, and all the other systems of nature as "ecosystem services."

He explains, "If humanity were to try to replace the free services of the natural economy with substitutes of its own manufacture, the global GNP would have to be raised by at least $33 trillion."[9]

"Ecosystem Services" Provided for Free by Nature

1. **Water treatment plants:** Literally. The more trees and plants in an area, the cleaner the water: "… forested watersheds capture rainwater and purify it before returning it by gradual runoffs to the lakes and sea," p. 107.

2. **Fertilizers:** With a little patience and planning, farmers can leave a field alone for a few years and it will produce more abundantly than it could with chemical fertilizers, which, by the way, have long-term harmful effects on soil and crops. — Leviticus 25

3. **Food:** We mainly depend on corn, wheat, and rice, but there are more than 30,000 edible wild plants, 10,000 of which can be cultivated in agriculture. Many of them can grow in more arid conditions, p. 114. What's more, with the pollination services provided by bees and other invertebrates, we depend on God's animals to keep these crops growing.

4. **Flood Control:** Plants and trees soak up excess water that could prevent property damage: "When 20 percent of the trees in the [Atlanta] metropolitan area were removed during its rapid development, the result was an annual increase in storm water runoff of 4.4 billion cubic feet. If Atlanta were to build enough containment facilities to contain this volume, the cost would be at least $2 billion. In contrast, trees replanted along streets, yards, and available parking space are a great deal cheaper," p. 108. These trees also serve to control erosion and prevent mudslides.

---

9 Edward O Wilson. The Future of Life. (New York: Random House, 2002), 106-119.

5. **Medicine:** Of all the pharmaceuticals on the market, 40 percent draw from extracts from wild plants, microorganisms, and animals, and not just for antibiotics, p. 119. We have only begun to unlock the healing power of God's creatures. He gave certain creatures the natural ability to control disease and we can mimic that in medicine.

Without a doubt, a healthy creation benefits all of humanity. Just take medicine, for example: 40 percent of new drugs come from natural sources. Wilson describes how scientists found an extract from a rare yucca tree that could halt the progression of HIV, and a poison-dart frog whose venom was a revolutionary painkiller. You name the illness, and researchers seem to be working on a nature-sourced drug for it! Isn't it ironic, though, that we will raise millions of dollars dumping buckets of ice water on our heads (as we did in 2014 to fund the ALS foundation) or walk 60 miles to find a cure for breast cancer, but then turn around and order our companies to bulldoze entire ecosystems, some of which may possibly contain the cure we are hoping for? As Wilson explains,

> **It is no exaggeration to say that the search for natural medicinals is a race between science and extinction, and will become critically so as more forests fall and coral reefs bleach out and disintegrate. p. 123.**

Although a healthy planet benefits all of God's children, some of us depend on it much more directly than others. Some people (myself included) have the luxury of depending on the planet *indirectly*. The indirect-dependers, if I may call them that, are those who typically would not be classified in Jesus' "least of these" category, in view of the numerous options available to them.

In pursuit of their ideal lifestyle these "most" are not always satisfied with their lot, so they buy, plough, dig, cut, slash, and burn their way through creation's resources. The resulting damage is no big deal to the "most;" they can just move away if things get too dirty. Meanwhile, those without the resources to relocate are left behind to survive the consequences, with their hardships compounded by the loss of creation services in their region.

Think about it. Who are the ones who:

> Buy property near landfills because that's all they can afford?

> Work in the dirtiest factories, making all the odds and ends we buy?

> Drink the ground water contaminated by mining?

> Live next to the smokestacks, polluting their bodies?

> Live in areas more prone to flooding due to low-lying locations and deforestation?

The list goes on and on, while the indirect-dependers just move away to greener pastures, blind to the wake of destruction they are leaving behind.

Examples from Our Past

Time and again throughout history, we have seen this scenario play out. Let's look at a few examples from our not-too-distant past that highlight the issue.

Dust Bowl

In the 1920's, a booming economy and rising stock prices pushed the price of wheat to its highest point on record. All across the Great Plains of the Midwest, farmers ploughed over the ancient grass ecosystems to plant more and more and more acres of wheat. The prices kept rising, so the farming industry kept expanding.

The year 1931 saw the onset of a drought for the region. This was nothing new to the Great Plains as droughts had come and gone periodically for millennia. The roots of the old indigenous grasses ran deep, so they were well equipped to weather the dry season. Wheat, on the other hand, was not. All across the Midwest wheat crops began to wither. With the soil no longer held by grasses, dry ground lay exposed to the open air. Strong winds picked up this dust, creating massive plumes of sand, silt, and dirt throughout the region. The dust storms came again and again, growing bigger and more intense as the drought waged on.

The citizens of the region with the funds to move away escaped to California or other parts of the country. Those who were unable to leave, whether for financial or other reasons—the "least of these"—were stuck behind in dust.

The consequences were horrendous. Food and water shortages led to health problems. Dust piled up like snow banks around many buildings, causing work and school to grind to a stop. Many of the region's residents contracted a unique kind of pneumonia due to prolonged dust-inhalation. The suffering went on for years until finally the rains returned.

To prevent a recurrence of this catastrophe the federal government purchased nearly four million acres of land in the Midwest and designated them "national grasslands." That helped a lot, in that particular instance. However, other environmental concerns last much longer than just one dry season and cannot be solved with one legislative act. Sometimes destruction can cause irreversible damage that can affect entire populations, even entire nations.

Haiti

Arguably, nowhere else are the poor suffering more from environmental destruction than in Haiti. According to HaitiPartners.org, Haiti is one of the poorest nations in the world, with more than half of its 9.7 million people living in extreme poverty, on less than $1 per day.[10]

---

10 "The Opportunity," Last modified 2015, https://haitipartners.org/

Things weren't always this bad. Art and Jocele Meyer have traveled all over the world to some of the poorest countries in their humanitarian work. They explain, "Haiti was once a tropical paradise, rich in land and natural resources. Thirty-two percent of its land was arable, compared with 14 percent worldwide. It had abundant rainfall and some minerals," p. 171.

Tragically, however, over the past several centuries, "colonial powers and multinational corporations, in collusion with the local elite, have exploited this land and its people mercilessly ... They continue to extract the last traces of natural resources (timber, charcoal, minerals, cattle grazing) from the land." The Meyers' powerful experiences after their first trip to Haiti inspired them to write the following:

> ...it is overwhelming to see the destruction of forests and land. Forests are gone and are replaced by deserts. Rain water is not retained; rushing water on steep hillsides erodes soil, forming ugly gullies. Reservoirs fill up with silt ... Without forests, arable land, and water resources, the base of the rural environment was degraded. There they found increased misery. To control these desperate and disillusioned people, political repression increased. Without food and employment, hunger and poverty escalated (173).

The Meyers argue that Haiti stands as an example or microcosm of what can (and will) happen to the "least" all over the planet if greed for natural resources is left unchecked.

The Slow Fade from Progress to Poverty

Haiti may be an extreme example, but many other countries around the world are slowly creeping in the same direction. The humanitarian organization Heifer International highlighted their work in Ecuador in the Fall 2014 edition of *World Ark* magazine. Some of their work centers on "defending the mangroves" to help struggling communities that depend on them for food and income. Mangroves are trees that live in brackish water (part salt, part fresh) along coastlines. Looking like an "overturned bowl of spaghetti," mangroves serve as unique breeding grounds for fish and shellfish, providing lots of little places for developing fish to hide from predators. Since so many species go there to breed, entire communities can live off the fish and shellfish found around mangrove trees. As Carmen Obando of Heifer International explains,

> Not much excitement on the surface, but in the water and among the branches teem an abundance of birds, fish, crabs, and other species that make mangroves one of the most diverse and productive ecosystems on Earth. Beyond providing habitat, mangroves stand firm against sea swells and storms, protecting the inland. They also clean salt from marine breezes, filter salt from brackish water and prevent erosion by holding soil in place with their roots.[11]

World Ark reports that when Flora Gomez moved to a seaside community in Ecuador 16 years ago, 60 families lived on that tiny island and sustained themselves entirely off the food collected in the mangroves and had enough left over to sell at the market. Over time, however, the seafood industry of Ecuador bulldozed most of the mangroves to make room for shrimp aquaculture. Now Flora's mangroves are fragmented and polluted. Flora has to search for hours to find a few of the shellfish that were once abundant, while wearing rubber gloves to protect herself from the skin-irritating shrimp farm waste. Flora's family is one of only a few still remaining in the community.

It's a story that's becoming all too common around the world. In his moving essay "Loving the Earth is Loving the Poor," Gordon Aeschliman put it this way:

> **And here's the harsh reality for the poor: it's usually their resources we are capturing to support our lifestyle, and their land, rivers, and lakes where we are dumping**

---

11 Carman Obano, "Defending the Mangroves," in *World Ark*, Heifer International, Fall 2014.

our waste. Quite literally, the poorest of the earth live on wealthy people's garbage.[12]

Whether the indirect-dependers (again, myself included) realize it or not, every action we take, every choice we make, no matter how small, has a consequence of some sort. It isn't likely the elite economic powers of Haiti's past *intended* for widespread destruction to happen. They were answering to their constituency and consumer demands. Thus, in reality the people *behind* the scenes were ultimately responsible for the destruction, hunger, and poverty, through their demand for resource-destructive goods. Again, Gordon Aeschliman said it best: "The true cost of living the modern lifestyle is not measured by what we pay at the cash register. Rather, it is measured by what we have done to other people's rivers, valleys, oceans, and land. And, more precisely, what we have done to the poor" (I-94).

Heal the Land to Help Them Stand

To address world hunger and poverty effectively, churches, Christian organizations, and mission groups need to adjust their methods to reflect the complicated world in which we live. The Samaritan in Jesus' parable did not just put a Band-Aid on the man in the ditch. He focused his care on the man, met his immediate needs, and employed the innkeeper for help. Essentially, the Samaritan stuck with the man until the problem was solved and he could stand on his own again. With today's deep-rooted problems and multi-faceted issues facing the needy, we need to change our tactics. Heifer International, the humanitarian group described earlier, takes a balanced approach to bringing people out of poverty—an approach that includes improving the environment, self-reliance, and improved animal management as "cornerstones for just and sustainable development." Heifer supplies livestock, plants, orchards, and starts farms in impoverished communities all around the world. At the same time, they also educate

---

12 Gordon Aeschliman, "Loving the Earth Is Loving the Poor," in *The Green Bible: Understand the Bible's Powerful Message for the Earth,* New York: Harper Collins Publishing, 2008, I-91-94.

farmers on best agricultural practices and sustainability. This multi-faceted approach not only gives the community food but also helps the poor become more self-sufficient for the long term. Heifer International works with government groups and local businesses to restore the wild areas that nourish impoverished communities. By working to protect and restore the mangroves in this coastal community, Heifer International not only helps to bring people like Flora Gomez out of poverty, but also preserves that community's way of life.

The problem isn't just lack of food or just lack of medical care or just lack of water. The real problems are the reasons *behind* those deficits. Simply treating the deficits is a step, but it is not enough if we are going to truly love our neighbors. It's time to come together, think creatively, and address problems at the source as we stand side by side with scientists and other groups that have the power, experience, and education to help us.

What Should Christians Do?

Once again, the "most" among Christians have done a great deal to help and support the least over the past 2,000 years. There is no denying that our work has brought glory to God in a powerful way through our efforts to help hurting people. But what if we're missing something that was never an issue before modern globalization—before the definition of "neighbor" began to change? How should Christians adjust as a result?

If it really is true—and I believe it is—that the definition of "neighbor" has changed, then, every Christian must examine his or her own actions, habits, and purchases in light of that new reality. We cannot justify reaching out our hands to the poor while making choices behind closed doors that hurt them: buying the shrimp from Ecuador that destroyed Flora Gomez's mangroves, or the coffee grown where rainforests once stood; or throwing away recyclable materials without

117

a second thought to the people forced to live next to landfills.

Jesus talked about separating the sheep and the goats—those who help the poor and those who don't—in Matthew 25: 31-46. In terms of the way we live our lives, some of us are—perhaps unknowingly—living like "goats in sheep's clothing." We help the poor when they're right in front of us, while insisting on the ability to live life—and buy stuff—on our own terms. Henry David Thoreau noticed this contradiction in the 1800s when he said, **"…it may be that he who bestows the largest amount of time and money on the needy is doing the most by his mode of life to produce that misery which he strives in vain to relieve."** Perhaps you didn't know that those imported shrimp you just bought last week were causing such damage to Ecuadorian coastal communities. Perhaps you cannot afford the more expensive wild-caught shrimp. I understand. But we cannot continue on our current track in good conscience if we want to serve the least.

***

A healthy creation is the biggest blessing we could give the poor and needy, not to mention our children and grandchildren. The next chapter expands on the notion of how the things we buy—and, more importantly, our *perception* of the things we buy—can either support or hinder our cause as followers of Christ.

Tink, Tink, Thunk

In a fourth-floor boardroom overlooking New York City's Central Park, a businessman waits on an important sales pitch. Pacing nervously around the 15-foot mahogany table, he is oblivious to the park's summertime glory outside the floor-to-ceiling windows. The boardroom chairs catch the sun's reflection flashing off his perfectly polished black patent shoes, as he fidgets through his note cards, quietly rehearsing every carefully crafted word.

Everything he has done the past five years has led up to this moment: his countless hours at the office, the baseball games he has missed seeing his son play, the weekly date nights with his wife he has given up, and all the other sacrifices he has made in preparation for today. Last week his wife expressed concern over his absence (again). He reminded her (again), "If I can just get this one sale, I'll get that promotion I've been waiting for, I'll buy us that sailboat, and I'll take you and the kids down the coast like we've always talked about." And now his wife's "too little, too late" response rings in his ears as he rounds the 20th turn of the boardroom track. Shaking it off, he reminds himself to "Focus!"

A glimmer of light off his watch catches his eye as he paces along the windows. He has three minutes until the meeting is scheduled to start. "OK," he says aloud to himself, "I'd better sit down so they don't see me pacing." Suddenly ... TINK. A flash of red and a loud noise draw his attention away from his note cards. He turns toward the window to see a beautiful male cardinal fluttering on the other side of the glass, looking stunned, with his scarlet head jerking around in an attempt to understand what just happened. The cardinal's bright red feathers stand in stark contrast to the blue sky behind him ... TINK. The bird flies into the window again.

"We can't have this distraction during the meeting," the man says to himself, so he removes his gold plated pen from his breast pocket and taps on the glass to try and scare the bird away.

THUNK ... This time the bird hits the glass with such force that the man is surprised the bird remains conscious. Then it dawns on him: the bird sees the reflection of the sky and the park in the glass and thinks he is just flying over the trees as usual. Feeling a flash of empathy toward the creature, he forgets all about the meeting momentarily, and he begins shouting and waving his arms and banging his fist on the window: "This isn't the park! Stop!!"

A fourth time the magnificent cardinal moves as though he were about to "tink" into the glass, but this time he stops, inches in front of the window. For a few brief moments, he just flutters there at eye level with the man as though staring past the reflection of the park and straight at him. Then suddenly an unexpected question flashes through the man's mind: **"Who's the one chasing an illusion?"**

CHAPTER SIX

Chasing Illusions

Our cup overflows, but we demand more cups

OK, I need you to do one thing before we continue:

If you are in a safe place and able to do so, please stand on one foot. I know it sounds strange, but it will make sense later. I promise. If you're reading this while riding the subway (for example) you are exempt, but if you can safely do so, put the book down, get up, and stand on one foot for as long as you can. I know you feel silly, but do it anyway. Seriously. Put. The. Book. Down.

OK, on with the chapter (and thank you).

***

We've all heard the ads that say, "Buy this car and people will treat you like you're important," or "If your husband really loved you, he'd buy you this jewelry," or "Buy this furniture and impress your friends." It seems that from the moment we wake up until the time we go to sleep, we are bombarded with messages trying to make us discontent.

Christian pastors have attempted to counter this discontentment with sermons about the dangers of greed and materialism. If you're a Christian, your pastor has probably unpacked scriptures on seeking first the kingdom, treasures in heaven, and countless other pro-contentment, anti-materialism lessons. You've probably heard that it's OK to have material possessions as long as they are kept in their proper place.

One thing your pastor may not have shared, however, is how the consequences of materialism can be far-reaching on creation. In our selfish acquisitiveness, we fail to see how many resources have gone into this car, how many streams have been clogged with silt from strip-mining to find that gold, how many rainforest trees have been sacrificed to get this mahogany.

Deep down we probably know our behavior has consequences, but we set aside that awareness and ignore the Bible's wisdom as we dig deeper, pave farther, and strive for more wealth, more status, and more stuff, scooping deeper and deeper out of the finite natural storehouses God has set up for all of us.

In other words, our cup overflows, but we demand more cups. We look at how prosperous those around us seem and suddenly one overflowing cup doesn't seem enough. As a result, all of creation suffers (including humanity).

This chapter will discuss how when we reach beyond our cup and give in to discontentment, we drain creation of its resources and end up more miserable than when we started. In choosing contentment, we find true freedom and ease creation's burden.

The Scramble for More and the Consequences on Creation

Quietly, desperately, we seem to scramble for more, more, more in modern society. When all is said and done, however, the Bible says we will end up doing more harm than good. No bank account, new car, gold jewelry, or any other material possession can give us what we're looking for. True security only comes from God, and we need to put our faith and trust in Him (for more on this see Proverbs 1:17-22, 11:28, 23:4-5; Matthew 6:19-21; Luke 12:16-20, 16:10-13; and 1 Timothy 6:9-10, 17-19).

Chasing after more, more, more leads us to take on a "MINE-tality:" an insatiable, selfish mindset that ignores the consequences of our behavior on creation or other people. King Solomon spoke of the folly of materialism in Ecclesiastes: *"Vanity of vanities, says the Teacher, vanity of vanities! All is vanity. What do people gain from all the toil at which they toil under the sun?"* (1:2-3).

So this brings us to another question. What would the world look like if *all* Christians simply followed these biblical instructions? What if every person on Earth who calls him or herself a Christian put his or her faith in God first and not in wealth or stuff or anything of this world? How would the world be different? How many social, economic, political, and personal problems would be solved automatically?

One thing I can tell you for sure: creation would benefit immediately. Since every single material possession comes from the storehouse of God's creation, every time we are discontent and want more, we take more from creation's resources. In that sense, the amount of God-fearing trust in the world may correlate inversely to the amount of greed, selfishness, and pride.

I think it is human nature to crave security. Perhaps God designed us with that drive so that we would ultimately be drawn to Him. All too often, though, we have to hit rock bottom to realize that the world's message of work, work, work, for more, more, more, will never be enough. In reality, all this striving for stuff only holds us back from experiencing God's will in our lives.

True Security

So what are you saying? Do you want us to stop providing for our families and go live in the woods? No, that's not what I'm saying. It's good to save money. It's good to work hard to provide for your family. The Bible speaks of both of those things as well (Proverbs 13:11). But that is not your first line of strength if you are a child of God.

To illustrate the point, imagine that your life is one long hike through a dark wilderness. Your material possessions are like the backpack you carry. If you have the light of the world inside you and walk in righteousness, God's Word will be a *"lamp unto your feet and a light unto your path"* (Psalm 119:105) guiding you right where you need to go. You have peace of mind, confident that God will show you the way and take care of you. Sure, there may be a time when you stumble and need to pull a Band-Aid out of your bag. That's what it's there fore. The key here is that the backpack is merely a *tool* to help you along God's path.

Now imagine another hiker who does not have this light within. She walks in darkness. Fear of the unknown weighs on her heart. How will she prepare for her hike? *Who knows?* she may think. *Anything could happen. I'd better be prepared for it all. I'd better bring extra bandages, hydrogen peroxide, anti-inflammatory drugs, extra food.* Before she knows it, her pack weighs ten times more than it needs to weigh. It's more of a burden than a helpful tool, and she wears out more quickly. Without the light of the world as a lamp unto her feet, the heavy pack causes her to stumble more frequently than the first hiker.

Likewise, when we store up treasures on Earth or seek worldly things first instead of the Kingdom of God, we accomplish exactly the opposite of what we set out to do. There's nothing wrong with the hiker having the backpack in the first place. What *is* dangerous is for the hiker to collect more in her pack than she needs. It's equally bad for her to withhold supplies from other worn-out or wounded hikers she passes, simply because she "might need the stuff one day."

Hikers who use wisdom and prudence as their guide, who keep their trust in God instead of their material possessions, are the "good soil" that Jesus talks about in the Parable of the Sower: *"These are the ones who, when they hear the word, hold it fast in an honest and good heart, and bear fruit with patient endurance"* (Luke 8:15). As a result, they "produce a hundredfold," or to continue with the analogy, they can hike a hundred times farther down the path.

On the other hand, hikers traveling with overloaded packs are the thorny soil. They may hear the Word, but *"as they go on their way, they are choked by the cares and riches and pleasures of life, and their fruit does not mature"* (Luke 8:14). They don't travel nearly as far down the path as they would have without all that gear weighing them down.

Here's the bottom line. True security doesn't come out of your proverbial backpack: your stuff, your wealth, your success, etc. True security comes from the confidence of knowing where to put each footstep as you are led by God. Not even a whole camping supply store could protect you like that!

This is what Proverbs 3 means when it describes how wisdom and prudence will guide you to walk securely on your way:

> *Happy are those who find wisdom, and those who get understanding, for her income is better than silver, and her revenue better than gold. She is more precious than jewels, and nothing you desire can compare with her. Long life is in her right hand; in her left hand are riches and honor. Her ways are ways of pleasantness, and all her paths are peace … Then you will walk on your way securely and your foot will not stumble. Do not be afraid of sudden panic, or of the storm that strikes the wicked; for the Lord will be your confidence and will keep your foot from being caught.*
> —Proverbs 3: 13-26

Jesus says to put our treasure in heaven. What does that mean for us? Freedom. Freedom from the need to find our own security. Freedom from wealth addictions. Freedom of knowing our steps are guided by the Lord. As Proverbs 11: 28 says, *"Those who trust in their riches will wither, but the righteous will flourish like green leaves."*

And what does that mean for creation and the poor? Relief. If we place our trust in God and take less from the storehouse of creation, there will be more to give to the poor and less of a burden on creation.

Choosing Contentment is Choosing Freedom

OK, so how do we get there? How do I break the bonds of my false-security addiction? How do I store up treasures in heaven and seek first the kingdom? The Bible has an answer for that too: Contentment.

Consider the following verses from the New Testament:

> *Of course, there is great gain in godliness combined with contentment; for we brought nothing into the world, so that we can take nothing out of it;* **but if we have food and clothing, we will be content with these.**— 1 Timothy 6:6-8

> *And the crowds asked him, "What then should we do?" In reply he said to them, "Whoever has two coats must share with anyone who has none; and whoever has food must do likewise." Even tax collectors came to be baptized and they asked him, "Teacher, what should we do?" He said to them, "Do not extort money from anyone by threats or false accusation, and* **be satisfied with your wages.**"— Luke 3:7-14

> **Keep your lives free from the love of money, and be content with what you have**; *for he has said, "I will never leave you or forsake you." So we can say with confidence, "The Lord is my helper; I will not be afraid. What can anyone do to me?"*— Hebrews 13:5

> *Not that I am referring to being in need; for* **I have learned to be content with whatever I have.** *I know what it is to have little, and I know what it is to have plenty. In any and all circumstances I have learned the secret of being well-fed and of going hungry, of having plenty and of being in need. I can do all things through him who strengthens me.*
> — Philippians 4:11-13

(Emphases added)

Contentment is a way of saying to God, "I know my needs are met by You. I trust You to supply me with everything I need." When we worry, in contrast, we are essentially saying, "What if I can't pay the bills? What if I don't have enough food?" Or really: "What if God doesn't come through?" Such doubt separates us from God.

Doesn't contentment contradict the illustration in Chapter 1 with the home and the Joneses? No. Like the hiker with the appropriate backpack, or Kenna using blankets to keep warm, there is nothing wrong with creating safe, nurturing homes for our families. After all, that's what God did with creation, isn't it?

There is a time and a place for owning our own material possessions; they just need to keep their proper positions in our hearts: below God, below our families, below our neighbors, and even below God's creation, which blesses and nourishes all. Godly contentment changes us and refocuses us on what is most important. As Dr. Calvin DeWit explained in his book *Earthwise*:

> Being content helps us personally, and it helps preserve creation's integrity. All the things we use, all the things we make, everything we manipulate, everything we accumulate derives from creation itself. If we learn to seek godly contentment as our great gain, we will take and shape less of God's earth. We will demand less from the land. We will leave room for God's other creatures. We will be responsible stewards, caretakers, keepers of creation. We will regularly allow creation to heal itself and perpetuate its fruitfulness, to the glory and praise of its Maker. (78)

Contentment Strategies

Contentment is a noble but challenging state to reach. I'm like many of you; I'll admit, I've struggled with greed. Although I'm still far from perfect, I'd like to share two practical steps to getting on the right path: Purchase "contentment insurance" and commit to doing a "world detox."

Contentment Insurance: We buy "insurance" for almost everything: health insurance, car insurance, home insurance, personal property insurance—all of which I own, by the way, and definitely recommend to you. But there's one recommended insurance policy that you may not have. This insurance comes with no deductibles, no co-pays, no confusing language, and when you really think about the alternatives, the premiums are really quite reasonable: only 10 percent of your income. I'm talking, of course, of tithing.

I like to look at tithing as purchasing "contentment insurance" or "greed protection insurance." Tithing is bringing 10 percent of your wealth back to the storehouse of God as a statement of gratitude, faith, and devotion to Him. That monthly payment is a reminder to yourself that you choose to believe what the Bible says, and you choose to trust God. By taking that step of faith, you give God the authority He deserves to have over your heart. The act says, "I know that money isn't my first line of defense. God is in charge of my life. God calls us to tithe in the Bible, so I will obey. He will always meet my needs, and I will be content with what I have."

Financial expert and best-selling author Dave Ramsey put it best when he said, "When you loosen your grip on money, money starts to loosen its grip on you." Giving has a wonderfully healing effect on the greed and materialism in your soul.

World detox: You have probably heard the saying, "You are what you eat." This mantra points out that much of your overall health and well-being is determined by your diet. The same is true for your soul, only your soul does not "eat" physical food. Your soul is nourished (or sickened) by what you see, hear, say, and do. Everything around you leaves an impression on you for better or worse.

If you're feeding your soul a lot of junk in terms of what you see (violent programming or pornography, for example), what you hear (negative talk, inappropriate language, and so on), what you say (cutting others down, fighting with your spouse, and all the destructive things we can do with speech), and what you do (concerning which the Bible has many long lists of advice and warning), then your soul will start to feel like a "junkie." Many people in this situation turn to more of the same to make them feel better, but it only makes things worse.

If your soul has been fed toxic "world food" for so long, you probably need a world detox to get you back on track. Fortunately, we are surrounded by opportunities to check ourselves in to what could be called "world-rehabilitation facilities," also known as churches. It may take some time spent searching to find the right one, but when you do, you will start to feel better, guaranteed. The church's success rate for rehabilitated "patients" is very high.

"But church is only on Sunday. What do I do the rest of the week?" Here are some tips:

Get into God's creation: Take the earbuds out and go for a walk just enjoying creation—the sights, smells, and sounds. Let all of God's masterpieces remind you what's really important.

Read your Bible: Open up God's word and spend time reading and praying. This is some of the very best "food" you can give your soul. You'll be amazed at the difference regular time with God in His word and in prayer can make in your life.

Remind yourself to be content: When you feel greedy or self-indulgent, fight off those feelings by speaking one of the contentment verses aloud. Or simply remind yourself: *I have everything I need. God is taking care of my family and me. I am content.*

Assess your soul food: Most of all, do an inventory of your "soul pantry" and clear out as much junk as possible. How do you know what is and isn't junk? Ask one question: Would Jesus approve? In any and all situations in life—the radio stations you listen to, the programs you watch, what you just said to that coworker who's driving you crazy—do you think Jesus would approve? If Jesus were sitting in your passenger seat, and he had just heard what's coming out of your car stereo, would you rush to change the song? Or would you sing it out alongside Him? If Jesus appeared next to you on the couch at night, would you scramble for the remote to change the TV channel, or would you turn up the volume?

If you would feel ashamed if Jesus appeared, then it's safe to say the item in question is a part of the world's junk food. If not, then you're probably feeding your soul with God's nourishing, joy-sustaining, and contentment-ensuring food. Once you clear out enough of your "soul pantry" you'll start to see the difference. Just like regular junk food drags you down, junk soul food saps you of your energy.

But when you feed your soul what it needs—encouraging speech, prayer, wholesome programming, time in nature, worship, and time in God's word—you feel rejuvenated, energized, and "awake" as Jesus instructed.

The Balancing Act

In a world that constantly tells us to buy, buy, buy, more, more, more, it may feel like you're standing on one foot being bombarded from all sides. All Christians must walk on a godly path that is "in the world, but not of the world." Sometimes we drift toward acting a little more "of the world" than we should as we let the pressures of this world get to us.

Well, let me ask you a question: How did you do with the balancing exercise at the beginning of the chapter? I'll bet you've been wondering when I would get back to that. How long were you able to stand on one foot? Unless you do it frequently, standing on one foot can be tricky. Your muscles flex this way and that as you try to keep from tipping over.

I happen to know a thing or two about such balancing acts. I ran track when I was in middle and high school. I remember how the team would always stretch out as a group before practices or meets. The quadriceps stretch was always a challenge because you had to stand on one foot to do it. I struggled with this when I was new to the sport, constantly losing my balance and stumbling over.

Finally, a friend gave me an unusual tip. She said, "Pretend you're holding onto an imaginary tea cup when you stand on one foot. It'll help." Incredibly, it did. Give it a try and see for yourself. (I won't hassle you this time.) Stand on one foot and hold an imaginary tea cup between your index finger and thumb. Did it help?

Pretending to hold the imaginary tea cup takes your mind off of the fact that you are balancing. It demonstrates an important truth: it's not that you are incapable of standing on one foot without falling over; it's your fear of falling that makes you lose balance. Look at the flamingo, for heaven's sake. They sleep on one foot!

In this materialist world, learning to live with the contentment that Paul describes in Philippians 4 is a lot like trying to stand on one foot — on a rocking boat. This world tries to knock you off balance; to buy into the lie of gotta-have-more-more-more. Your muscles flex this way and that as you try to maintain your upright posture. Your fear begins to grow. You lose your sense of security. Soon you find yourself making unnecessary purchase after unnecessary purchase.

Fortunately for us, however, we have a good friend who gives us the key to the balancing act. When you are fighting against the materialistic world and trying to keep your treasures in heaven, your relationship with God is your teacup — except in this case it's real, not imaginary!

I know it sounds strange, but go with me here. Just as in the track analogy, it's not that we are incapable of walking the fine line between having stuff and trusting God. It's our fear of falling that makes us lose our balance. Just as the imaginary teacup took your mind off the fact that you were balancing a moment ago, and enabled you to balance for longer than before, God's presence can do the same. The stronger your relationship is with God, the more trivial and less desirable the things of this world will appear to you. You do not notice the balancing act as much.

In other words, when you take time to build your relationship with God by spending time in prayer and reading God's word every day, the pressures and noise of the world gradually start to melt away. After all, "if God be for us, who can be against us?" Now that is true security!

In the beginning, you might stumble or have to put your other foot down, but after a while, the balancing act isn't so hard any more. If you stick with it, reading the Bible consistently, meditating on it, and bringing your concerns before God with supplication and thanksgiving, then *the peace of God which surpasses all understanding will guard your hearts and minds in Christ Jesus.* (Philippians 4:7)

Now imagine that ALL Christians did this. I believe many (if not all) of our environmental problems would be solved automatically.

***

The businessman in the boardroom at the beginning of this chapter asked a very important question: "Who's the one chasing an illusion?" The answer is: both of them. Both the man and the cardinal were focusing on a false or unreal world. The bird was focusing on the false park reflected in the glass. It looked just like the park. It looked like it would provide everything the bird needed: shelter, nourishment, security … TINK.

The man was focusing on the false world of materialism and power. The things of this world looked like they would bring him everything he could need. Just this one more sale … TINK. Just this one more promotion … TINK. If I can only make a little more money, then I'll be happy … Both the bird and the businessman were deceived. Both were only hurting themselves. Both needed to turn completely around and focus on the real "real world" of God's kingdom.

Are you chasing illusions of security?

The final chapter of this book will describe the shift that needs to occur in the Body of Christ if we are going to enjoy God's creation the way it was meant to be enjoyed, protect natural resources that support "the least of these," and give glory to God by protecting His master-pieces.

The Tale of the Middle-Aged Geologist (Part Two)

"Why didn't I take the petroleum job?!?" Jamie asks himself for the fiftieth time as he boards a small plane on the edge of the Amazon Rainforest. Jamie is a graduate student working a summer geology internship with the Mega Citrus Produce Co. He had chosen the paid citrus internship over the unpaid petroleum internship purely for financial reasons. He had no particular interest in citrus, but he did have a load of student loan debt and some high credit card balances.

He'd made that painfully obvious in his internship interview, so he'd been surprised to be offered the job a week later. Now, boarding the plane with envelopes full of "hush money" to give to local indigenous people, it's starting to make sense. Mega Citrus is aggressively pursuing the acquisition of 200 acres of rainforest habitat, and the only thing standing in their way is a small tribe whose only claim to the land is that they just happen to have lived there for the past 20-plus generations. Mega Citrus had had good luck with hush money in previous land acquisitions. Now they needed a more detailed geographic analysis of the area, so they had asked Jamie to go.

Jamie, for his part, simply cannot wait to get back to civilization. He loves geology—he'll happily spend whole afternoons collecting rocks and studying landforms—but he is definitely not the camping type. This is going to be camping to the extreme, he knows, and he dreads the idea of spending a week sleeping on a mat under a mosquito net.

The flight takes twelve grueling hours. Finally they land on the remote airstrip, where the pilot leaves them, heading back to Rio until his scheduled return a week later. Jamie studies the map with his two guides and his interpreter. Not being the patient type, Jamie feels his insides reeling toward low-level panic as his guides debate whether the village is here or here or here on the map. Worse still, the "guides" (he's beginning to wonder if they could even be called that) realize that they brought the wrong GPS devices, not yet fully recharged from the last expedition. "Don't worry," they reassure him, "We should be there by nightfall."

Knowing he has no choice, he tries to sound chipper: "Okay, that sounds great." Notebook and pen in hand, he follows his guides and interpreter into the rainforest.

Hours go by without a single human being in sight. Jamie's anxiety escalates. "What if we never find this village? What kinds of animals live out here?? WHY didn't I take the petroleum job!!?!" Two o'clock comes and goes. Three o'clock. Four o'clock. Five o'clock ....

By 6 o'clock they're all exhausted and arguing over where to set up camp, when a small boy with two dead rabbits hanging over his shoulders appears. The boy had heard their argument, and was wondering what the strange sounds were. Everyone is immensely relieved to see other signs of human life.

The interpreter jumps into action to explain their situation to the child. The boy's dialect isn't familiar to him. Jamie's impatience grows as they struggle to communicate. At last they succeed in getting the basics across, and the boy agrees to help them find the village.

After a while, Jamie finds himself thinking, "This kid is amazing." No more than 10 years old, he maneuvers barefoot through the thick brush of one of the wildest places on earth as easily as Jamie would walk down a crowded sidewalk. Jamie has a half brother, Michael, about this age, but all he ever sees is the back of Mike's videogame-immersed head in front of a screen when he goes to visit. "Michael wouldn't last 10 minutes out here. This kid is alone and miles away from his home in the deepest darkest jungle *and* is bringing food home to his family."

They arrive at the village after dark. The young man, they learn, is the tribe leader's grandson. Jamie is invited to stay in the tribe leader's hut with the family. The next day, he delivers the envelopes and other gifts from the company. Normally, they would head back to the airstrip at this point, but no one in the tribe knows the way except for a few who are out on a hunting expedition. Fully discharged by now, the GPS is useless to them. They have to rely on the radio to communicate with the Brazilian authorities, line up another plane, and, they hope, get back to civilization. As one guide attempts to amplify the signal with a length of wire attached to the antenna, the only thing the rest of them can do is wait. And wait.

Over the next several days Jamie spends hours with the young man who led them through the forest as the boy follows him around out of curiosity. Jamie teaches him (through sand-drawings and hand motions) about the rocks around the village. The young man shows him a few edible plants. Jamie makes a little ball out of vines and teaches him how to play hackie sack. The boy shows him a few tribal rituals including traditional greetings and farewells.

To his surprise, Jamie finds himself growing fond of him. After a few days, Jamie gives him a little puzzle that he had brought along, a small and colorful circular maze with a tiny ball bearing inside, tied to a string so it can be worn as a necklace. Overjoyed, the boy rushes off to show his friends.

Watching this boy show the other children the puzzle, Jamie begins to feel a twinge of sadness for the villagers. He knows what's coming. Upon his return to Tampa, he'll deliver his report, and the rest of the process will fall into place for the citrus deal. He realizes in that moment just how much the thought bothers him. He has grown to care for these people.

Just then, a sudden great shout goes out from a villager on the edge of the village announcing the hunting expedition's return. The village explodes with excitement as the hunters are welcomed back and catch up on the week's events. One hunter agrees to take Jamie and his crew back to the airstrip in the morning. The boy insists on accompanying them.

They set out at daybreak. A trip that took a full day with the "guides" in the lead only takes a few hours with this knowledgeable leader. The plane is there when they arrive. Jamie turns to the boy and their hunter-guide. Unable to look them in the eyes, he gives them their customary tribal goodbye far more awkwardly than he had learned it, utters a quick thank you and boards the aircraft.

As the plane lifts off from the ground, he leans his forehead against the window to see the two villagers watching from below. "They'll be fine," Jamie tells himself, "It won't hurt them to join the rest of civilization, anyway."

***

Ten years go by. Jamie has by now become a product line manager within Mega Citrus. He flies back to Brazil for meetings about another piece of tribal land. The tribe's lawyer picks Jamie up from the airport, and they set out for the meeting at the firm's Brazilian headquarters.

After a surprisingly short drive, the lawyer pulls up to a river bank lined with ramshackle huts made predominantly of cardboard, plastic, and sheet metal. "What in the world are we doing here?" Jamie protests. "This isn't where the meeting is!" The lawyer simply answers that there is someone there who wants to speak with him and insists that Jamie get out of the car.

Walking up to the cardboard village, they approach a group of men sitting in a circle of dirty white plastic lawn chairs. One man stands and faces Jamie. "Do you remember me?" he asks in broken English, through yellowish, sunken eyes looming over protruding collar bones. Jamie has no answer until the man pulls on a string around his neck and reveals the puzzle Jamie had given to the boy in the village all those years ago. The man Jamie had known as a boy, who is now in his twenties, looks twice that age now (at least.)

Through the lawyer's interpretation, Jamie learns that the tribe had come here to live after being evicted from their land. Their extensive knowledge of the rainforest had proved useless in the city. More than half the tribe had died due to drinking water and eating fish taken from the contaminated river. Citrus operations upriver were responsible for the pollution.

Looking into his old friend's eyes, Jamie knows that he is in large part to blame for their suffering. He could have gone back and told the executives the soil was too rocky or the gradient too steep to bother planting their groves. They would have believed him and dropped their pursuit of that land. But no. He had told them how fertile the land was, and how it was surrounded by two rivers perfect for irrigation. So they had pushed out this tribe that had been there for longer than anyone could remember. This was the tribe that had kept him alive and shown him kindness. This was the young man who had guided them through the rainforest to safety. He would have had a family by now. But he barely has the strength to stand.

Deeply shaken, Jamie realizes he has a very hard decision to make now—and yet not so hard, since there is only one right answer. He goes to his meeting, where instead of finalizing the land acquisition deal, he retracts it, with tears of regret for his previous mistake.

He knows his job is over, and indeed Mega Citrus fires him immediately upon his return. Haunted by the catastrophic effects his actions have had on this wonderful group of people who showed him remarkable kindness, he decides to become an activist for indigenous people's rights. Now he travels the world staging sit-ins and protests.

He'll even go as far as sleeping on a sidewalk in front of corporate offices—which is where a well-dressed wedding guest who mistakes Jamie for a homeless man accidentally kicks Jamie on his way to the church, and they strike up a conversation.

***

The wedding guest sits wide-eyed as he hears Jamie's tale, transfixed by those mesmerizing eyes. Jamie tightens his grip on the young man's arm as he makes his final and most important point:

> *Farewell, farewell! But this I tell*
> *To thee, thou Wedding-Guest!*
> *He prayeth well, who loveth well*
> *Both man and bird and beast.*

> *He prayeth best, who loveth best*
> *All things both great and small;*
> *For the dear God who loveth us,*
> *He made and loveth all.*

CHAPTER SEVEN

Keeping Creation Good

We can do all things through Christ who strengthens us

Doesn't it seem that we always think we have everything figured out? Yet time and again God has revealed different aspects of His character to guide us from glory to glory. In the earliest years, for example, Christians struggled to come to terms with the old, legalistic traditions of Judaism. Paul and other pioneers of our faith guided them through those questions and gave clarity about God's grace. The church's place in government was another point of contention throughout history. Some Americans distorted Bible verses to justify slavery prior to the Civil War. Each of those times the Christians in question thought they were doing right.

It's happened over and over again: the history of Christian doctrine is filled with error, dispute, discovery, and recovery. God showed us our errors, and we've grown through them. Each correction along the way has challenged us to come up higher and grow a little closer to being the bride of Christ that we are supposed to be. Like a woman preparing for her wedding, we've ironed out some of the wrinkles of the past, smoothed off the rough edges of our bad choices, and little by little, adorned ourselves in the flowers of righteousness.

I think we have come to another step in this bridal preparation process. It is time now for a shift in our thinking if we are going to enjoy creation and not exploit it, right some of the wrongs we have done, preserve the visible manifestations of God's glory in nature, and protect natural resources to support the least among us. Making

143

big changes is always difficult, but we can do it. This final chapter will suggest a simple step that I believe will tip Christians toward creation care. But first we need to understand the nature of the change we need to make. Allow me to demonstrate through a familiar analogy.

Talking Cells

To begin, I'd like to ask you a question: What if the cells in your body could talk to you? What would they say? Would they give you a high approval rating, or would they protest your misconduct? What do you think a lung cell would say to a smoker? In his letters to early Christians, Paul explained how each one of us serves a unique purpose in the world as members of the Body of Christ:

> *For just as the body is one and has many members, and all the members of the body, though many, are one body, so it is with Christ ... If the whole body were an eye, where would the hearing be? If the whole body were hearing, where would the sense of smell be? ... As it is, there are many members, yet one body ... If one member suffers, all suffer together with it; if one member is honored, all rejoice together with it.*
> — 1 Corinthians 12:14-26

These verses help us appreciate one another and grow together for the betterment of God's kingdom. However, when Paul wrote the verses about the Body of Christ in his letters (Romans 12:5, 1 Corinthians 12:12-31, Ephesians 1-4) the little building blocks of life known as cells had not been discovered yet. If they had, I imagine Paul would have included them, too; so if I may, allow me to expand on Paul's analogy for a moment.

Each one of us is like a tiny cell in the body of Christ. And since cells make up tissues, tissues make up organs, and organs make up organ systems, we come together in various facets of Christianity to do the work of God in the world. As individuals, we (cells) come together in Bible studies, prayer groups, and Sunday school classes to form little communities (tissues). All those small groups work together within the framework of a church (organs). Churches come together to form denominations (organ systems). Finally, even though denominations may squabble sometimes, we are followers of Jesus in the end, so Christian denominations come together to form one organism, or the Body of Christ.

But we can continue the analogy even further. **The blood of this body is God's mysterious and wonderful creation.** Think about it: blood is the medium that carries life-giving oxygen to every living cell, contains all the nutrients needed for survival, and helps cart away waste materials. Creation gives us air, food, water, and everything else we require while removing the waste materials from inside of us. If that life-giving blood stopped going to even one cell, tissue, organ, or organ system, it would die. If the blood contained toxins or carcinogens, all of the organs would begin to feel the effects.

So this begs the question: if creation is the life-blood of the body of Christ, how is the Body doing in its collective health maintenance? Does the Body have the energy and stamina of an exuberant healthy youth, ablaze with enthusiasm and purpose? Or has the Body started to become a little sluggish? Have the toxins started building up in our systems, sapping us of our former stamina? Have some organs begun to falter, even as others continue to run at full steam?

Look at what happens to smokers. Nicotine is one of an estimated 400 different toxins in cigarettes. When the waste materials reach a tipping point and the body has more toxins in it than its blood is capable of expelling, the consequences start to fall into place. At first, only the respiratory system is affected (perhaps). Later on, as emphysema and other illnesses set in, the blood brings less and less oxygen to the rest of the body, causing all other organ systems to begin to feel the effect: fatigue and sluggishness at best, cancer and death at worst.

My point is this: what are we doing to ourselves on the large scale with our pollution, habitat destruction, and the like? As with a smoker's nicotine addiction, are we harboring unacknowledged addictions of greed and materialism? Have the byproducts of these addictions

145

(pollution and creation destruction) begun to affect our performance as a body?

I'd like to reiterate how the Body of Christ does tremendous work around the globe: feeding the hungry, clothing the poor, curing people in hospitals, and serving to help with the countless other concerns that plague humanity. But let's face it: We are also part the problem. As Pope Francis said in his *Top 10 Tips for Bringing Greater Joy into your Life*: "I think a question that we're not asking ourselves is: Isn't humanity committing suicide with this indiscriminate and tyrannical use of nature?"[13]

In a sense, I am just a lung cell calling out, *"Wait a minute, here. Why are we content with poisoning ourselves, destroying creation, and hurting the poor? Surely we can figure out a better way! Just look at all of our astounding accomplishments over the past 2000 years. I mean, you name it, and it seems like we've done it! Can't we get together and figure out a solution to this creation destruction problem too?"*

The Real Curse

Many of us are still blind to our addictions and their damaging effects on the Body. Worse still, we are training our children to act as we do. This reminds me of a story from my past.

As a child I went to a summer camp called the Green River Preserve, which had a mountaintop area of open bare rock called Lower Bald, looking out over the beautiful rolling hills of Appalachia. When we would hike up to Lower Bald as campers, our leaders would often ask us to just sit quietly, looking out over the landscape. These peaceful and serene moments in God's creation had a tremendous impact on my life.

About 10 years later, someone had built a house on one of the mountains across the valley. When I attended GRP's 20th anniversary

---

13 Pope Francis, *Viva*, July 27, 2014

celebration, the sight of that house made me intensely angry. My eyes were immediately drawn to it—the one thing that didn't belong. I knew the homeowner had every legal right to build that house, but that didn't stop it feeling wrong to me. The landscape seemed tainted. The campers and mentors that were there with me were angry too. Let's just say things were said that I will not repeat here.

That was more than a decade ago. Today's campers are accustomed to the house being there. They have no idea what they're missing. The view is still beautiful, for sure. But only those who knew the way it was before can understand or appreciate how much has been lost. Some campers even speak of how they wish they lived in that house, so they could have a view like this for their very own. Mentors do their best to try to explain how much better it could have been if it had been left natural, as more and more houses keep popping up.

***

Environmentalists often talk about how angry future generations will be with us. Our children will turn to us one day, they say, when environmental problems have passed the point of no return; they will accuse us, saying, "You had the opportunity to do something about habitat destruction, water pollution, and species extinction. And you didn't! Why?" That day may come. But I think something even worse is more likely.

Just as new campers accepted the house on the once unblemished landscape, future generations will accept God's creation the way the previous generations left it for them. We get used to the little blips on the horizon and come to accept them without question. Then little blips turn into bigger scars and, gradually, monstrosities that render the landscape unrecognizable. And we don't even know what we're missing.

In other words, **the real curse to future generations is an inheritance of apathy**; not a pile of environmental problems to deal with, but a "whatever" attitude combined with destructive habits.

Honestly, I would prefer anger over indifference. Anger leads to action. Indifference leads to more of the same. Rather being outraged at the destruction of God's creation, we're teaching our children our excuses and how to add to the destruction. We're training our children to poison themselves with pollution, ignore the effects on the poor, and to accept creation destruction as "the way things are." So what should we do?

Creation Care Tipping Point

A change in the way we treat God's creation will follow a shift in our ethics. The question then is, what will cause our ethics to shift? In his brilliantly inspirational book *The Tipping Point: How Little Things Can Make a Big Difference*, Malcolm Gladwell describes how major shifts in thought tend to happen. Gladwell analyzed why some trends "take off" and others seem to fade out quickly.

After studying everything from diseases to fashion trends to educational movements, Gladwell discovered a pattern. In every instance, seemingly small actions by a special group of people at the right time and place caused the successful social movements to "tip" and catch on among the masses with astonishing results. He describes how a small group of trendsetters started a major trend in fashion circles, one television producer caused literacy rates to climb nationwide, and a simple police strategy caused crime rates to plummet in New York City. As Gladwell explains in the book's conclusion,

> But if there is difficulty and volatility in the world of the Tipping Point, there is a large measure of hopefulness as well.... In the end, Tipping Points are a reaffirmation of the potential for change and the power of intelligent action. Look at the world around you. It may seem like an immoveable place. It is not. With the slightest push—in just the right place—it can be tipped.[14]

---

14 Malcolm Gladwell, *Tipping Point: How Little Things Can Make a Big Difference*, Back Bay Books, 2002, 259.

Working off Gladwell's theories, I would like to propose a similar small step to help Christians tip from pro-God, anti-creation to creation-caring out of love for God; from hurting the least with our everyday choices to serving the poor with all actions; from "we'll-get-a-new-one-anyway" apathy to respect for God's master-pieces; from "what's-in-it-for-me?" self-centeredness to "then sings my soul, how great Thou art"; from an inheritance of apathy to respectful creation stewardship.

The simplicity of the step may surprise you: church recycling bins. If every major church in the US, and especially the Southeast, would place recycling bins in the main sanctuary next to trash cans, in plain sight of congregants and use them to recycle unused church bulletins and other paper, I believe that simple step could shift our patterns toward God's creation.

This simple, seemingly insignificant step serves as a powerful symbol. Think about what a recycling bin communicates, especially since recycling is still optional in the U.S. When you see a recycling bin on the curb in front of your neighbor's house every week, what does that tell you?

Without saying a word, those neighbors are demonstrating how they care. They're willing to take the time to separate their trash, rinse out glass containers, check plastics for the right numbers, break down cardboard boxes, and go through all the other steps needed to get that bin ready for pick up. Conversely, putting all one's trash in one bag communicates something entirely different.

I'm not asking you to judge your neighbors by their trash bins. We can't know why they do what they do unless we ask them. But it is undeniable that recycling bins send a message—one that essentially says *we care*. Perhaps your church already does this. That's great. But not all do. When we moved to our new house here in Georgia, we visited more than a dozen different churches to find a new church home, and only one—Sugarloaf United Methodist Church—had recycling bins in prominent locations.

Now, think about this: what would it communicate if every church across the nation had recycling bins next to every trash can? I think it would tell the world we care about God's creation, and we've committed to taking a small step to preserve the resources God has so graciously bestowed on us.

The pastor could communicate *why* the bins were going in next to the trash cans. Even if he or she did not do that, though, and just installed them without fanfare, I believe that small step could be the tipping point for Christians' views on conservation. The nascent movement would generate new leaders from within, who then would raise new awareness about the issues and make changes within their church and home. Eventually, I believe real large-scale change might happen.

Now, if you're a pastor and if the idea of recycling bins next to every trash can sounds like too big a step, or if you are worried about what your congregation would think, I'd like you to try a little experiment for me.

Just put out *one* paper recycling bin near the main entrance with a comment box. Include a little sign saying: "We're thinking of starting a recycling program. What do you think? Feel free to make it anonymous, but share your name/email if you'd like more information." Then see what comes in. I bet you'll be surprised at the positive feedback.

Next, share your thoughts with the respondents via email to encourage a dialogue on the topic. If you decide to go ahead with a church wide paper recycling program (which I think you will), you could ask the commenters if they'd be willing or interested in serving as the church's "creation task force." They could look for ways to improve church energy usage, coordinate litter cleanups, or do any number of things.

As Tri Robinson says, "there are people who are consummate lovers of creation in every church. Getting these people on the ground floor of developing an environmental ministry in your church is vital to your success" (127). By the way, Robinson's book has some great money generating suggestions for the church, such as his "Tithe your

Trash" campaign and mobile phone recycling. Check out *Saving God's Green Earth* for more information.

***

The task before us is a difficult one. The problems facing God's creation are tremendous, perhaps even overwhelming. But if Christians were to shift their perspective on creation, that could make all the difference.

As discussed in Chapter 4, change may start off slowly: throwing trash out of your car window doesn't feel like a good idea; you find yourself recycling more and more; you get in the habit of bringing those reusable bags to the grocery store. Then you may start making more conscious choices: You think about imported items you're about to buy and what kind of impact that could have had on the local people.

Just imagine if every Christian made this shift. I believe many of the problems facing our planet would be solved automatically. As Bruce Babbit once said, "If the two most powerful forces in America, religion and science, could be united on the issue, the country's environmental problems would be quickly solved." (See Wilson's *The Future of Life*, pp. 159-160, for more on this.) If we tackle the small things, perhaps the big things will take care of themselves.

I promise, it'll be worth the effort. Tri Robinson describes how committing to creation care was like "discovering an untapped vein of gold" for evangelism, and has opened doors within the community he never knew were possible.

Consider this testimonial of his community's reaction:

> From the moment we began promoting and modeling caring for God's creation as a value in our church, there has always been such enthusiasm by our people and favor within the community. Someone donated a billboard to us. Someone else gave us a box truck that we painted our environmental ministry logo on the side and used it to transport recyclable goods to a local recycling facility.

> Throughout all the time I've spent in full-time ministry, I've started many ministries, but I've rarely seen the supernatural hand of God make things happen like He has with this particular project.
> *Saving God's Green Earth,* 75

***

Samuel Taylor Coleridge wrote *The Rime of the Ancient Mariner* in 1797.[15] Ever since, scholars have argued over its main message. Briefly, the *Mariner* is a story about a sea voyage gone wrong, told by a sailor seeking his fortune. Why this mariner chose his occupation is unclear, but what is certain is his disgust for marine organisms. At one point in the beginning, he looks down the side of the ship and curses all the "slimy creatures" he sees in the water.

Then, after spending some time aboard the ship, the crew becomes stranded in a dead calm. Weeks without wind go by. The ship and the crew begin to run out of supplies. All hope seems lost. Suddenly, an albatross appears, soaring over the ship. Since albatrosses can fly for hundreds of miles without stopping, they are considered birds of good fortune or omens of good luck.

The mariner's shipmates are overjoyed. The sailors see this bird as their saving grace that came just in the nick of time before they were about to succumb to dehydration. However, for unknown reasons, the mariner kills the bird with his crossbow. Horrified, the other sailors curse him and make him wear the albatross around his neck. When the winds remain idle in the following days, they blame him for their suffering, and they begin to die off one by one. The mariner is the only one to survive.

Finally, something changes in the mariner's heart. After weeks of isolation, at the brink of starvation, crippled by dehydration, the mariner looks down the side of the ship once more at the sea creatures below. Only this time, instead of cursing them as slimy and detestable, he "blessed them unaware."

---

15 Samuel T. Coleridge, *The Rime of the Ancient Mariner,* Ontario: Dover Publications, 1970.

As this unexpected sentiment grows within him he begins a new relationship with God's creatures, and learns to love and respect the natural world. In this transformational moment, the albatross falls into the sea, and another ship arrives to rescue him. As penance for his deed, the mariner must wander the earth, telling everyone his tale of the importance of God's creatures.

You may have read this famous poem in grade school and discussed its literary significance. If your school experience was like mine, the discussion probably ended there.

But this 200-year-old poem is arguably more relevant today than it was when Coleridge wrote it. There was plenty of creation abuse 200 years ago—reading a few pages of Callum Roberts's *The Unnatural History of the Sea* will show you that.

Compared to today's widespread habitat destruction, species extinction, and global pollution, though, the actions of our pre-industrial-revolution ancestors seem innocent and trivial. Now more than ever, we need to realize the main message of that poem:

> *He prayeth well, who loveth well*
> *Both man and bird and beast.*
> *He prayeth best, who loveth best*
> *All things both great and small;*
> *For the dear God who loveth us,*
> *He made and loveth all.*

The story about the wedding guest in San Fransisco prior to the introduction of this book and that of Jamie and Mega Citrus at the beginning of this chapter combine to be a modern day version of this famous poem. Only this time, Jamie's albatross is an entire ecosystem and the consequences reach much farther than just one ship full of sailors.

***

Perhaps, we all have a few albatrosses among the skeletons in our closet. These are items or actions causing irreparable damage or destruction to an aspect of God's perfect creation. Again, some damage and destruction is inevitable in a world of sin. This is true. We cannot be as perfectly in tune with nature as the rest of creation like we were in the Garden—at least not until Jesus comes back. But does that make it OK to expand our skeleton-closets to accommodate a growing number of albatrosses? Definitely not. So what do we do?

***

Remember . . .

We can (and will) do all things God calls us to do through Christ who strengthens us!

The task before us may be difficult, but it is *far* from impossible. God cares deeply for His creation, His masterpiece, and He watches over every detail. He is the owner of all creation, but He put us in charge of its day-to-day operations (Chapter 1). We *can and will* treat creation justly if we humble ourselves and examine our "enjoyment" of creation in its proper light (Chapter 2).

We *can* break the addictive cycle of selfishness and greed in our lives and begin to free creation from bondage. At Jesus' second coming, the children of God will *know* how to care for creation, so creation will finally be able to sing its new song of joy. I know that we most certainly *can and will* live like we are already in the New Heaven and New Earth (Chapter 3).

By the grace of God, I believe we *can and will* recognize how precious creation is to God: a place where we grow as individuals, thrive in our work, learn more of God, and draw closer to Him. Without a doubt, we *will* recognize the Biblical value of nature (Chapter 4).

I believe we *will* stop living like goats in sheep's clothing when it comes to our choices in creation that hurt the "least." I believe Christians all over the world *can and will* examine what it means to be a "neighbor" in the 21st century to answer Jesus' call to help hurting people (Chapter 5). Like the ancient mariner, we *can and will* put aside our own selfish ambitions and greed and choose contentment instead (Chapter 6). Lastly, I believe we *can and will* take steps to address our greed and materialism addictions to prevent the "real curse" of an inheritance of apathy (Chapter 7).

***

When Christians really care for creation, there will be no end to the good we can do. We will find cleaner energy sources. We will stop habitat destruction. We will preserve God's wild places. We will provide clean water, clean air, and clean soil to our children and the "least of these" that are so important to God. And most of all, we will do all these things to the glory of God and the benefit of the Kingdom.

At this moment, I ask that you go to God in prayer. Read the critical verses from the introduction again, reflect on the parables of the past seven chapters, and ask God what He thinks. Ask Him if there's anything in your life that He wants you to change. Ask Him to reveal what you might be doing to harm His creation or hurt the "least." And most of all, ask Him for the courage to follow through with whatever He tells you to do. In Jesus' mighty name.

To God be the Glory.

AFTERWARD

A letter of gratitude to my most honorable stewards holding dominion over creation.

Dear friends,

Once again, on behalf of all creatures great and small, I, Ruban Quercus, wish to inform you of our joy over your decision to reclaim your proper positions over creation.

Yes, our suffering is great right now, but our new song waits just below the surface for the glorious day when Jesus returns and frees us from our bondage. We sense that day is near, and your decision marks a shift in the pattern of destruction toward our promised hope.

You see, even though we put forth thorns and thistles to protect ourselves now, we always have and always will love you dearly. As I mentioned in my first letter, you are creatures like us, but made in the image of God and blessed with the awesome power of free will. Despite our best defenses, we are still devoted to you, because that's what God wanted. We are meant to be a blessing to you, and I'm glad you now realize that blessings from God should never be wasted.

In the Garden, we did what we creatures were created to do: work day and night as God's master-pieces designed to give his most precious children a safe and nurturing home where they could grow, learn, play, and love. Even now we have not given up hope that more and more of you will choose to reclaim your proper position as just stewards over creation. We hold on to the hope that you will do your part to rule over us fairly, preserve us diligently, and glorify God mightily in the process.

I know many of you doubt your own capabilities in this respect. So before I go, I would like to remind you of the very highest compliment mankind has ever received. This compliment is often overlooked in the Bible because it was given in the midst of great evil you were doing.

In Genesis 11, as God examined the Tower of Babel, created by humans who intended to become like God as a mode of transportation to heaven, He said the following: *"Nothing that they propose to do now will be impossible for them."* Wow. Of course, God was not thinking these actions were good by any means, but think about the implications... The creator of the universe said that about you! Incredible.

Because your great power to do so much was coupled with your fallen sinfulness, He chose to scale back your capabilities. He scrambled your languages so that you could not finish the job. Now with modern technology, unlimited transportation, and global communication systems, you are so much more interconnected than even just 20 years ago. Just as it was with the Tower of Babel, nothing you propose to do will be impossible for you now, be it for good or evil.

Your sinfulness remains real, and great power remains a source of great temptation. However, by the grace of God and through the strength and power of our Lord and Savior Jesus Christ, Christians can take back creation.

You must unite to do that. Your decision today to reclaim your proper position in creation is the first and most important step that you will take for us.

Please encourage others to do the same so more will come back to us and enjoy all that we creatures have to offer. We are waiting for you...

All our love,

Ruban Quercus III

For more information on how to keep creation good including a small group curriculum, please visit:

www.keepitgood.org

APPENDIXES

Appendix A

Synopsys of The Rime of the Ancient Mariner

Three men are on their way into a wedding banquet when a strange old sailor stops one of them, grasping the wedding guest's shoulder and staring at him with piercing eyes. "Why did you stop me?" the young man protests, "I need to go into my cousin's wedding."

"There was a ship," says the strange man. The wedding guest tries to free himself from the old man's grip, but when he looks into this stranger's piercing stare, he finds himself utterly transfixed and is powerless to do anything but listen.

> *The Wedding Guest sat on a stone;*
> *He cannot choose but hear;*
> *And thus spake on that ancient man*
> *The bright-eyed Mariner*

The old mariner then begins a story of a sea voyage he took as a young man. He and his shipmates set sail from his homeport with everything looking promising and cheerful. However, a storm soon overtook the ship and blew it hundreds of miles off course, north past the Arctic Circle.

> *And through the drifts of snowy cliffs*
> *Did send a dismal sheen:*
> *Nor shapes of men nor beasts we ken—*
> *The ice was all between.*

But just when all seemed lost, a beacon of hope found them. A majestic sea bird known as an albatross, capable of flying hundreds of miles without stopping, began following the ship. They saw the albatross as a sign that their bad luck was about to change, so the men were eternally grateful.

At length did cross an Albatross,
Through the fog it came;
As if it had been a Christian soul;
We hailed it in God's name.

The bird proved to be more than a beacon of guidance, for a strong south wind to push the sails seemed to follow the bird. The sailors hailed the bird as a messenger from God.

However, not all the mariners saw the bird that way....

For a moment, the old mariner pauses in his story to the wedding guest. A far off look of utter horror and turmoil comes over his face as he envisions the next part of the story in his mind. The next part contains his deepest regret—the act that has plagued him for decades—the one thing that rends his heart, robs him of peace, and forces him to wander endlessly. Though frightened by what he sees in the mariner's expression, the Wedding Guest asks him:

'God save thee ancient Mariner!
From the fiends, that plague thee thus!
Why look'st thou so?'—With my cross-bow,
'I shot the ALBATROSS.'

The mariner gives no reason for committing such an atrocious act. Perhaps the act was driven by hunger from weeks at sea. Perhaps he was jealous of the attention the bird was getting. Perhaps he had no real reason at all. He may have been too ashamed to say. Whatever the reason, after he shot the albatross the other mariners turn on him scornfully. He killed the messenger from God—the guide, their hope, their shining light through the storm.

And I had done a hellish thing,
And it would work 'em woe:
For all averred, I had killed the bird

164

That made the breeze to blow.
Ah wretch! Said they, the bird to slay
That made the breeze to blow!

Not long after that, the wind and the sea became silent, the sails became still, and the men began to suffer from dehydration.

Day after day, day after day,
We stuck, nor breath nor motion;
As idle as a painted ship
Upon a painted ocean.
Water; water everywhere
And all the boards did shrink;
Water, water everywhere
Nor any drop to drink.

In the desperate delusion of their hunger and dehydration, their view of the world around them was altered. It seemed as if the ocean itself was rotting and all the slimy water creatures within it were evil:

The very deep did rot: O Christ!
That ever this should be!
Yea, slimy things did crawl with legs
Upon the slimy sea.

The other men placed full blame for their suffering on the shoulders of the Ancient Mariner. As penalty for his heinous act, and as a symbol of his shame, they forced him to wear the Albatross around his neck.

Just then "a flash of joy" sprang up inside the men as they spotted a ship on the horizon moving toward them. Then they realize it was moving without wind or tide. Fear gripped them even tighter. On board the strange ship were Death and Life-In-Death, gambling for the men's lives. Death won the lives of most of the men, but "Life-in-

Death" won the life of the Mariner. As a result, one after another, the crew succumbed to dehydration, but the Mariner lived on.

The souls did from their bodies fly—
They fled to bliss or woe!
And every soul it passed me by,
Like the whiz of my cross-bow!

Alone, the Mariner tried to pray for forgiveness or mercy, but found himself unable to, due to the evil still reigning in his heart.

I looked to heaven, and tried to pray;
But or ever a prayer had gusht,
A wicked whisper came, and made
My heart as dry as dust.

Day after day he lived on, surrounded by his dead shipmates. Night after night he stared at the moon and stars, yearning to travel to them but remaining ever still, always with his albatross hanging around his neck reminding him of his mistakes.

One night, he looked into the ocean and saw the same water creatures swimming around in the shadow of the ship against the moonlight. However, this time they did not appear to him like maggots in the rotting corpse of a dead sea. This time seeing them brought him joy:

O happy living things! No tongue
Their beauty might declare:
A spring of love gushed from my heart,
And I blessed them unaware:
Sure my kind saint took pity on me,
And I blessed them unaware.

In that moment of humility as he gave up fighting and began blessing God's creatures, finally, he became truly repentant. The curse of the

Albatross began to lift, and he was finally able to pray:

> *The self-same moment I could pray;*
> *And from my neck so free*
> *The Albatross fell off, and sank*
> *Like lead into the sea.*

At long last, the Mariner was able to sleep, blessed by the holy mother with gentle sleep that "slid into his soul." As he slept he dreamed it was raining; and when he awoke, the buckets on the deck were full with rainwater. God continued to bless the repentant Mariner by sending a troop of spirits to help him work the sails. Even though the seas were calm and the wind does not blow, they miraculously sailed on toward an unknown destination. Along the way, however, he learned that his penance for killing the albatross was not yet over, as he overheard two spirits talking about him:

> *"Is it he?" quoth one, "Is this the man?"*
> *"By Him who died on cross,*
> *With his cruel bow he laid full low*
> *The harmless Albatross."*

> *The other was a softer voice,*
> *As soft as honey-dew*
> *Quoth he, "The man hath penance done,*
> *And penance more will do."*

The ghostly ship sailed on and on until, to his utter and ecstatic joy he saw his home country port. The angelic spirit troop began to leave the ship. At that same moment, he heard the human voice of a Hermit on a small boat approaching the ship. As the Hermit and his pilot observes the strange-looking ship and approaches nearer, the ship suddenly began to sink. Weary and confused, the mariner did not even call for help, but the Hermit was still able to find and save him.

Like one that hath been seven days drowned
My body lay afloat;
But swift as dreams, myself I found
Within the Pilot's boat.

Back on firm ground again, the Mariner was struck with grief over his actions, and he begged the Hermit to shrieve him. The Hermit asked to hear his story and upon its telling, the pain the Mariner felt lifted.

Forth with this frame of mine was wretched
With woful agony,
Which forced me to begin my tale;
And then it left me free.

Ever since this moment, the Mariner walked on and on from land to land to retell his tale, over and over again. He does not know whom he should tell until he sees the chosen person's face:

Since then, at an uncertain hour,
That agony returns;
And till my ghastly tale is told
This heart within me burns.

The Wedding Guest and the Mariner hear the bells and songs of the marriage feast, but the Mariner is not quite finished. He tells the guest the real reason behind his wandering, the truth behind his punishment, and the one thing that will haunt him forevermore:

Farewell, farewell! But this I tell
To thee, thou Wedding-Guest!
He prayeth well, who loveth well
Both man and bird and beast.
He prayeth best, who loveth best
All things both great and small;

For the dear God who loveth us,
He made and loveth all.

The Mariner leaves. The Wedding Guest—though he is "next of kin"—does not go into the wedding banquet but leaves instead:

The Mariner, whose eye is bright,
Whose beard with age is hoar,
Is gone: and now the Wedding-Guest
Turned from the Bridegroom's door.

He went like one that hath been stunned,
And is of sense forlorn:
A sadder and a wiser man,
He rose the morrow morn.

Appendix B:

Sidney Lanier's *The Marshes of Glynn*

Glooms of the live-oaks, beautiful-braided and woven
With intricate shades of the vines that myriad-cloven
Clamber the forks of the multiform boughs, -
Emerald twilights, -
Virginal shy lights,
Wrought of the leaves to allure to the whisper of vows,
When lovers pace timidly down through the green colonnades
Of the dim sweet woods, of the dear dark woods,
Of the heavenly woods and glades,
That run to the radiant marginal sand-beach within
The wide sea-marshes of Glynn; -

Beautiful glooms, soft dusks in the noon-day fire, -
Wildwood privacies, closets of lone desire,
Chamber from chamber parted with wavering arras of leaves, -
Cells for the passionate pleasure of prayer to the soul that grieves,
Pure with a sense of the passing of saints through the wood,
Cool for the dutiful weighing of ill with good; -

O braided dusks of the oak and woven shades of the vine,
While the riotous noon-day sun of the June-day long did shine
Ye held me fast in your heart and I held you fast in mine;
But now when the noon is no more, and riot is rest,
And the sun is a-wait at the ponderous gate of the West,
And the slant yellow beam down the wood-aisle doth seem
Like a lane into heaven that leads from a dream, -
Ay, now, when my soul all day hath drunken the soul of the oak,
And my heart is at ease from men, and the wearisome sound of the stroke
Of the scythe of time and the trowel of trade is low,
And belief overmasters doubt, and I know that I know,
And my spirit is grown to a lordly great compass within,
That the length and the breadth and the sweep of the marshes of Glynn
Will work me no fear like the fear they have wrought me of yore
When length was fatigue, and when breadth was but bitterness sore,
And when terror and shrinking and dreary unnamable pain
Drew over me out of the merciless miles of the plain, -

Oh, now, unafraid, I am fain to face
The vast sweet visage of space.
To the edge of the wood I am drawn, I am drawn,

Where the gray beach glimmering runs, as a belt of the dawn,
For a mete and a mark
To the forest-dark: -
So:
Affable live-oak, leaning low, -
Thus - with your favor - soft, with a reverent hand,
(Not lightly touching your person, Lord of the land!)
Bending your beauty aside, with a step I stand
On the firm-packed sand,
Free
By a world of marsh that borders a world of sea.

Sinuous southward and sinuous northward the shimmering band
Of the sand-beach fastens the fringe of the marsh to the folds of the land.
Inward and outward to northward and southward the beach-lines linger and
curl
As a silver-wrought garment that clings to and follows the firm sweet limbs of
a girl.
Vanishing, swerving, evermore curving again into sight,
Softly the sand-beach wavers away to a dim gray looping of light.
And what if behind me to westward the wall of the woods stands high?
The world lies east: how ample, the marsh and the sea and the sky!
A league and a league of marsh-grass, waist-high, broad in the blade,
Green, and all of a height, and unflecked with a light or a shade,
Stretch leisurely off, in a pleasant plain,
To the terminal blue of the main.

Oh, what is abroad in the marsh and the terminal sea?
Somehow my soul seems suddenly free
From the weighing of fate and the sad discussion of sin,
By the length and the breadth and the sweep of the marshes of Glynn.

Ye marshes, how candid and simple and nothing-withholding and free
Ye publish yourselves to the sky and offer yourselves to the sea!
Tolerant plains, that suffer the sea and the rains and the sun,
Ye spread and span like the catholic man who hath mightily won
God out of knowledge and good out of infinite pain
And sight out of blindness and purity out of a stain.

As the marsh-hen secretly builds on the watery sod,
Behold I will build me a nest on the greatness of God:
I will fly in the greatness of God as the marsh-hen flies
In the freedom that fills all the space 'twixt the marsh and the skies:
By so many roots as the marsh-grass sends in the sod
I will heartily lay me a-hold on the greatness of God:

Oh, like to the greatness of God is the greatness within
The range of the marshes, the liberal marshes of Glynn.

And the sea lends large, as the marsh: lo, out of his plenty the sea
Pours fast: full soon the time of the flood-tide must be:
Look how the grace of the sea doth go
About and about through the intricate channels that flow
Here and there,
Everywhere,
Till his waters have flooded the uttermost creeks and the low-lying lanes,
And the marsh is meshed with a million veins,
That like as with rosy and silvery essences flow
In the rose-and-silver evening glow.
Farewell, my lord Sun!
The creeks overflow: a thousand rivulets run
'Twixt the roots of the sod; the blades of the marsh-grass stir;
Passeth a hurrying sound of wings that westward whirr;
Passeth, and all is still; and the currents cease to run;
And the sea and the marsh are one.

How still the plains of the waters be!
The tide is in his ecstasy.
The tide is at his highest height:
And it is night.

And now from the Vast of the Lord will the waters of sleep
Roll in on the souls of men,
But who will reveal to our waking ken
The forms that swim and the shapes that creep
Under the waters of sleep?
And I would I could know what swimmeth below when the tide comes in
On the length and the breadth of the marvellous marshes of Glynn.

Baltimore, 1878.

Additional Creation Care Resources

A Rocha International: Conservation and Hope: www.arocha.org

Evangelical Environmental Network: www.creationcare.org

Christianity Today: http://www.christianitytoday.com/ct/topics/c/creation-care/

Care of Creation: Pursuing a God centered response to creation crises: www.careofcreation.net

Au Sable Institute: www.ausable.org

Restoring Eden: Christians for Environmental Stewardship: www.restoringeden.org

About the Author

C. Lindsay Linsky lives with her husband and two children in Suwanee, Georgia. She grew up in Atlanta and studied Biology and German at the University of Georgia. After earning her Masters of Arts in Teaching at Emory University, Lindsay went on to teach Life Science and Reading in Atlanta Public Schools and Hall County Public Schools. After helping her middle school students develop a school-wide recycling program, Lindsay went back to graduate school for her PhD in Science Education from the University of Georgia. Her dissertation work centered on Ocean Literacy and the impact of a professional development program in Hawaii on 12 Georgia teachers. Currently, she works as an Assistant Professor in the College of Education at the University of North Georgia, Dahlonega.